Leila Berg

LOOK AT KIDS

Penguin Books

D1634549

LOOK AT KIDS

Leila Berg

Penguin Books

How can the bird that is born for joy
Sit in a cage and sing?
Blake

Penguin Books Ltd, Harmondsworth,
Middlesex, England
Penguin Books Inc, 7110 Ambassador Road,
Baltimore, Md 21207, USA
Penguin Books Australia Ltd,
Ringwood, Victoria, Australia

First published 1972
Copyright © Leila Berg, 1972

Made and printed in Great Britain by
Butler & Tanner Ltd, Frome and London
Set in Lumitype Baskerville
Designed by Stuart Jackman

A little of this material
has appeared in various
forms over the last few
years in the *Guardian*,
Anarchy, *Where*, *Teacher*,
The Times Educational Supplement.

1

In a doctor's waiting-room, a young father and mother had brought their very new baby. I saw the unsentimental shells of its ears, and its waving starfish fingers like something left stranded by the sea on a strange surrealist shore, an anemone in a pool. Then suddenly, as a shepherd hurriedly, shoutingly, pushes his flock through a gateway, the baby waved upwards, faster and faster, tempestuously flailing his arms with all his might – faster, faster – urgently shooing forth words towards the passionately working mouth that opened wide for a shout!

But the shout was soundless. Nothing. What was it the baby meant to say?

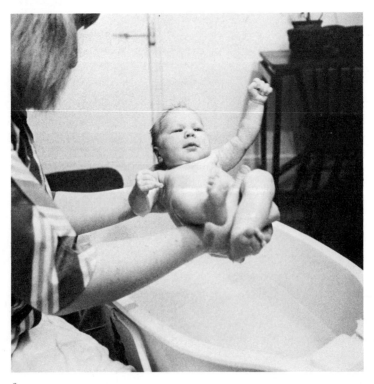

2

Babies are international. Lying in his cot, babbling as he grows, a baby speaks the consonants and vowels of every race in the world.

Energy galvanizes the whole of him, setting his body wriggling, his hands clutching, his legs waving and his tongue, lips and jaws babbling. He doesn't have to be taught to do this, any more than a bulb has to be taught to send up a shoot. His speech is part of his vitality. With every movement of every part of him he is sending something of himself into space, he is launching himself into the world.

Mmmm and *nnnn* he says, like a sexy woman, snuggling, desiring. And *p p p* and *d d d* he says, delighting in play. All over the world, mamans, mums, nanas and nannies, dads, pappas, pas and babushkas, we cry 'That's me!' and turn his expressive sounds into the role we choose to play, answering him. The baby is amazed, and delighted. He makes his magic sounds again and again, and again we exclaim with joy and admiration, identifying ourselves as his family, and he crows in shared delight.

Still international, he continues to explore all the other sounds he can make, joyously feeling out his abilities. But now he begins to notice when he has scored a bullseye. So he concentrates on the sounds these important adults like best, the ones they have chosen for their language, the ones they respond to ; and he practises them. He has plenty of time to practise. None of this – neither the rich exploration, nor the mutual response, nor the selection, nor the concentration – has been taught him.

He listens to tones of speech, and long before he can speak an English sentence speaks an English tune – or more accurately, the tune of English people who are important to him and who respond with delight. I used to listen to a one year old, the child of actors, pouring out his language with a rollicking delight, shouting with pleasure if you tossed it back to him, embroidering on it and wildly exaggerating like his father if you encouraged him, and like his father finally capping it by laughing uproariously – it seemed – at his own joke. Other times, also like his father, he talked very gravely, as if lecturing or conducting

7

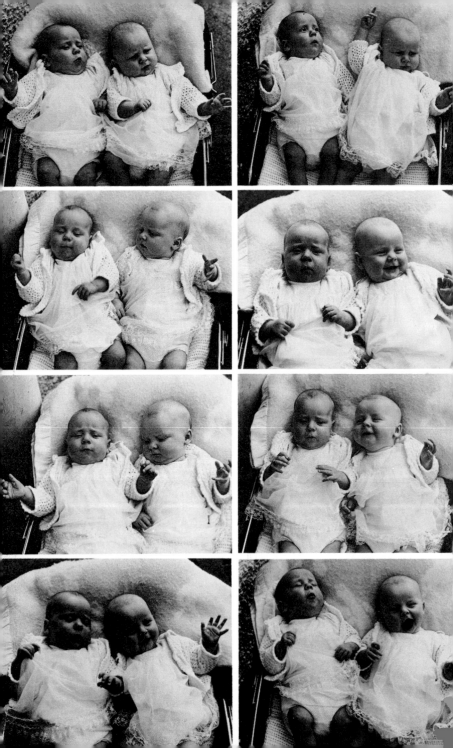

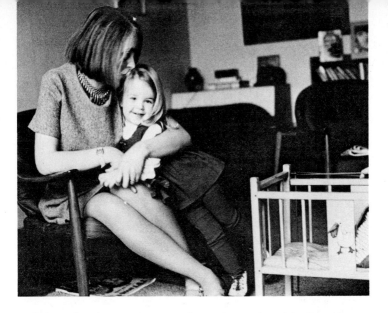

a philosophical inquiry, raising his eyebrows inquiringly at the
end of what sounded for all the world like a sentence, looking a
little haughty and aloof the while. He reproduced so accurately
tune, rhythm, expressions, gestures (like these pictured babies
who must surely know fishermen!) it was difficult to realize it was
an abstract work of art you were listening to.

So very gradually, since he is living in England, and since
therefore his parents have changed from their own international
infancy to an adult Englishness, the baby too becomes English.

Yet for some time he still holds on to his internationalism,
understanding other children emotionally even when he does not
understand their words (until eventually adults will tell him that
other people are foreigners and that they, the adults, are ill at
ease with them, even sometimes afraid of them, and that their
language and their ideas can only be learned, if at all, in a place
called school). There has been no theory in this growth of speech.
The adult has responded with pleasure to what the baby gives, and
shown the baby how to turn this pure joy into a tool of
communication. Something has been lost, but only in the sense
that one cannot have everything. The baby has given up belonging
to the whole world in exchange for a loving reciprocity, a
deepening of personal identity, a companionable apprenticeship.
And the whole structure has been built on the natural sounds of a
growing baby.

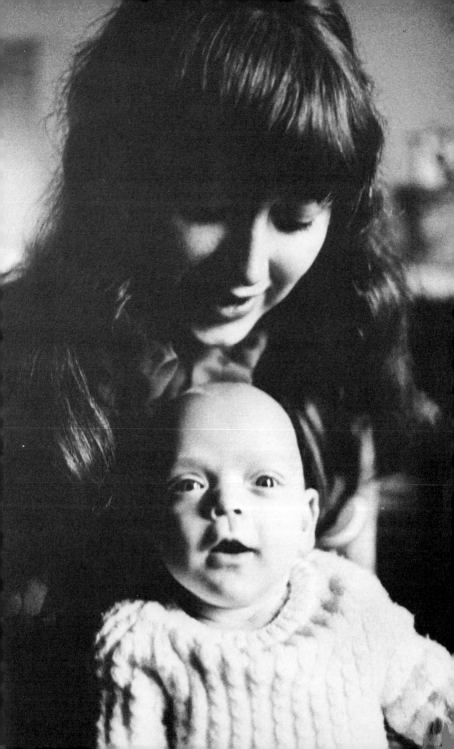

3

Down the street an old man shuffles past a pram. The baby babbles away. 'Shut up, you little bleeder!' says the old man with hate. 'Shut up!'

Two one year olds live very close to me. Whenever they start to talk their own language they are yelled at. 'Shut up!' 'Stop that row!' If they go on – slap! Sometimes they will try out one long sound – a slow gurgle or a pensive squeal. Then they are hit without the warning. Perhaps these sounds are irritating to a grown-up. But they are not intended to be – unless the grown-up refuses to share the delight; then, since a human being must have a response to keep sane or alive, the child makes do with a slap. A slap is often the only way an adult and a child communicate in London.

In the bus queue, a three year old was talking animatedly to her mother. The mother stared straight ahead, silent – until suddenly she exploded, her voice furious, detonating. *'That's all I ever get from you! – chatter, chatter, chatter!'* The little girl's lively intelligent face changed, and she looked wary, self-conscious, off-balance and silly. I wondered what else a mother expected to get from a three year old. What else has a small child to give? And what gift could one have that is more tender, more joyous, more remarkable?

I have often sat in buses near these trapped, resentful, desperate mothers, whose life has never belonged to them. They stare silent and stony-eyed in front of them, while the child chatters away asking for a response that is never forthcoming. The child stamps on the seat; then she bends right under her mother's face gazing upwards in one of those extraordinary curves of childhood, and says, 'Mum?' Still the mother stares straight ahead, rigid. The child fondles her face, turns her chin towards herself, with a mixture of tenderness that is waning through fright, of concern (for herself as much as for her mother), and a desire, half emerging, to pay back by pinching. Then the mother speaks. 'For God's sake, shut up!' she says.

All their reactions geared to overcrowding, to noise, to lack of privacy, to complaints, to demands, to chaos and loneliness, such mothers cannot even relax when they have space around them.

I once saw a seven year old out with her grandmother in Battersea Park. The little girl was wandering over the grass, absorbed in a song of her own that she sang meanderingly like a blackbird. I stopped and watched her. Her grandmother spoke, out of that enormous expanse of parkland. 'Stop that bloody row or you'll go home!' she said.

And in another bus queue I watched a little girl dancing, partnering her reflection in the dark shopwindow. She was not annoying anyone, she was well away from the queue and easily within calling distance when the bus came. But her mother yanked her and slapped her into submission.

Even on holiday, Londoners still carry their chains. In the Isles of Scilly, I watched two young couples on the grass talking excitedly about home movies. 'Here, remember that one he took at breakfast! We was all eating cornflakes!' 'Yes – and the wind was blowing!' 'What a scream!' 'The cornflakes –!' 'And he reversed the film!' Hysterical choking, followed by an absorbed, respectful assessment – 'That was clever!' 'That was a year, that was!'

Cutting into this, their unseen child calling from the distance, 'There's a tractor here!' Nobody moved. But the mother slightly turned her head to shout 'Get down!' and then father, happy of the chance to appear alert and efficient, jumped up and said, 'I'll get him!' and the mother called after the father, 'Tell him the lady says get down!' Around them English eyes looked downwards for no 'lady' had said get down.

Out of sight, the child, dealt with, wailed, 'Oh . . .' then resilient, and quickly excited again, shouted, 'Mum! Can I stroke the dog?' And the mother, not even moving her head this time, shouted, 'No! You stroked it last year!'

(Yet that same day, in that same place, I saw something completely different. A small sandalled girl, still a baby, aged about one and a half, stood outside a shop, pointing very excitedly down the street. ''ello! 'ello! 'ello! 'ello!' Her mother came out of the shop, and the child with tremendous excitement shouted again, still frenziedly gesturing. ''ello! 'ello! 'ello!' I thought she was greeting someone. But the mother looked the way the child was looking and said instantly, with identical pleasure and excitement, 'Oh yes! That little girl has yellow flip-flops just like yours, hasn't she!')

4

I sat among twenty seven year olds, sent from a local primary school, and asked them to help me write a story.

From the first impatient words, it was evident that Nigel was the kind of child who a few years ago would have been at a prep school. There was a great deal of power in his background, that masculine, mother-hating, mother-betrayed power; there was also a great deal of adult conversation. His feelings were very intense – they were mainly feelings concerned with power, a tremendous need to identify with powerful adults, scathing feelings towards those whom he hoped would prove inferior, a passionate egotism. (At one point, when he had held solo sway for a very long time, and was then offered a mild, brief and intelligent criticism by a little girl, he said, stuttering with passion, 'I don't care! It's not Amanda's story! It's *my* story and,' with a proud gesture to me, 'maybe it's *your* story, but it's not Amanda's story!; and I had to say gently that it was everyone's story.)

But absolutely concurrent with the power, indeed translating it from wishes to reality, was the mastery of words and syntax which made it so easy for him to manipulate ideas. He could work out a plot, plan for the future; he could take a leap away from known experience into a detailed unexperienced future; he could fight for his ideas – and he did.

He was not interested in human relationships – except in manipulating them – and had not mused much on their subtleties. It was Amanda and another girl (not with 'power' backgrounds) who pooh-poohed one point in his plot by saying that it would be the elder sister, not the mother, who would bossily cause trouble for the other children, because she was nearer their own age and this 'would make her *funny* with them'; this disconcerted him for a second but he did not consider it, and I think their wisdom, the result of accurate observation and awareness of their own experience, was quite lost on him.

His vocabulary and his skill were far in advance of the others; the only thing that impeded him was the very tumbling out of the words and ideas, that sometimes, so to speak, got jammed in the doorway and had to fight to break free.

I discovered before the children left that he always 'sat up to dinner' with his parents and their friends. One could imagine the talk that ranged round him, that seemed to him so powerful, into which he tried imperiously to join and in which he sometimes had to fight to gain, or hold, a place.

Other children in the group were very different. I remember one groping after his own idea that was already fading before he could find the words to claim it. He saw it for a second in all its glory – fireworks shooting out stars! – and before he could speak one halting sentence the radiance had dissolved into air and only the burnt-out stick and spent cardboard remained; he was bewildered, troubled, and faltered into silence. Two seven year olds, one already fluent and flaming with power, one already halting and crippled.

And yet, would the school rejoice if the second child reproduced his parents' speech, his parents' tune? Would they listen with pleasure as he recounted his true family experiences, and approve of them as no doubt they do of Nigel's very different ones? Would they lovingly reciprocate?

5

I stand by the railings in Battersea play-park and watch. In front of me is the brow of a green hill, littered with large play-bricks. A boy comes into view, from the left, about six years old. With some very definite purpose, he seizes a wheelbarrow full of bricks and starts to trundle it away. Just then, over the hill comes a three year old. He sees the older boy, and the wheelbarrow, and is riveted with the force of a lightning conclusion. Then his paralysis ends. He hurls himself at the other boy, kicks him, pummels him, tears at him. The older child is astonished. He drops the handle of the barrow, and does not know what to do. He is also very angry. He makes a decision. He strides purposefully towards a crate of bricks, with a porter's truck lying alongside. Grimly, resolutely, with his back to the small one, he begins to fill the truck with bricks from the crate and from the grass.

Again the little one is riveted, appalled. Again, after a minute's paralysis, he hurls himself, thundering over the grass, at the older one, and kicks him savagely, tearing at his clothes. And again the older one is furiously angry. His teeth are set, his face is black with murderous hate. He does not know what to do. Life has never brought him this problem before. He has tried to deal with it forbearingly, for after all he is not a baby; he has done his best, but it is unavailing. In a second he will turn on the little one and bring a brick crashing down on his head, annihilating him. But within that second the little one, quite unaware of doom, is suddenly entranced by the movement of the boy's hands, still grimly, fightingly, going from the crate to the truck, the crate to the truck; and caught up in the movement, in the rhythm of it, in the satisfying creative result of it, his flailing arms stop in mid-air . . . waver . . . and then swing also into the crate and the truck, the crate and the truck.

The older boy is amazed. But he says nothing. No recognition of any kind passes between them. He goes on filling the truck, and the little one does the same, puffing a little with exertion. When it is full, the older one straightens up, grips the handles, and wheels it off.

The small one stands up, startled again. A flicker of doubt passes over his face as he sees the boy and the truck and the bricks disappear. He had not foreseen this. He stands watching, uncertain, poised. Then with a sudden sturdy acceptance he turns, and trudges chubbily back over the hill, on some quest of his own.

Throughout the whole episode not one word has been spoken. Neither has acknowledged the other. It has only been movement – appearance, conflict, cooperation and exit – like ballet.

Now that was an extraordinary thing. I was ready to cry out – or rather, because the moment had that knife-edge delicacy when a sudden cry might bring catastrophe, I was on the point of calling with tensely gentle reassurance to both of them, 'It's all right.' But I held back. And it *was* all right. More all right than I could ever have made it.

Yesterday, Richard sat on the floor with me and we played picture
dominoes. I hadn't met him before; he's four. I showed him how
you stand your dominoes up so that only you can see them. He
picked the game up immediately. Then at one point, several of my
dominoes fell over. I hurriedly started to pick them up. But then
I saw Richard was looking at them intently. So I took my hand
away and let them lie; I even managed to knock over several more
in doing so. He gazed, very thoroughly. Then he chose a domino
from his own pile.

Authoritarians would assume he chose one that would block
me. Also they would say he was cheating. And also that I had
encouraged him to cheat. They would say 'man is naturally
competitive', and that is why we have to try to teach him not to
cheat, because if we didn't he would destroy civilization; and so
on.

But Richard didn't block me. He deliberately chose a domino
that would enable me to continue the game.

He did it not because he was altruistic, or self-sacrificing, but
because he needed the game to continue, he wanted our
relationship – our cooperation – to continue. To win – that is, to
destroy this pleasant relationship-in-existence – was an idea quite
alien to him. But an authoritarian adult would have taught him to
win – and to destroy what was important to him, and ultimately to
believe that winning was what he wanted.

I met Elizabeth and Judy for the first time at tea. Elizabeth nearly two, Judy four.

They sat at the table, and they each took a cream cracker. I offered Elizabeth the butter dish. She took some butter with her knife, an enormous lump. She put it on her plate, then picked it up in her hand and squashed it, squeezing it through the cracks between her fingers, gazing at it gravely, very much caught up in its texture and the crackle it made as it ballooned through.

I offered Judy the butter dish. She also took a very large lump with her knife. Made slightly apprehensive by Elizabeth, I half put out a hand to dissuade her, then stopped. She spread all her butter on one cream cracker, using her large knife very deliberately and carefully and with great pleasure. It lay very thick. Then she stretched her knife towards the butter dish again. 'But that's enough!' I started to say – and again I stopped. Carefully and skilfully she was scraping off the surplus butter from her knife against the side of the dish; then she scraped carefully and delicately and skilfully all over her cream cracker, removing more surplus butter, and returned that to the butter dish . . . and went on and on repeating this process till her cream cracker had a thin but absolutely smooth layer of butter on it. Sitting with great enjoyment bolt upright, and crooking her little finger, she nibbled with flamboyant style.

Elizabeth at two, sensuously exploring her material. Judy at four, carefully controlling a tool and practising a technical skill and a social skill. Neither of them was primarily interested in eating. If I had thought they were, I would have interfered and stopped them growing.

We are always extraordinarily sure that all that children are interested in is food – perhaps because that is all we are sure we can give them. And we can patronize them and ridicule them

while we give it – oh, in the nicest possible way – which makes us feel doubly secure. But even very deprived children are not *primarily* interested in food. I once knew some children like this, so deprived at three they did not even respond to their own names. One day – drawn by the activity of another child – they became absorbed for the first time in a game, pouring out water from a child's tiny tea-set and pretending it was tea. But they were expected by adults to be having real food and drink, because they were half-starved. And eventually, very gently, the make-believe tea was taken away from them (it had to be *taken* away, because the children would not give it up) and real food was set before them. They turned their faces away and would not eat.

Up till that day when they played their first game, they had wolfed the food down. Now they had found something deeper – and had it taken away from them. They ate nothing that day.*

* I have described these children and this incident in more detail in *The Tram Back* (Allen Lane The Penguin Press, autumn 1972, written with Pat Chapman).

A friend told me recently that she was watching a child build a sandcastle and not succeeding, and found herself very surprised the child didn't lose her temper; almost she decided to help the child. Much later, still thinking about the child's surprising self-control, she suddenly realized that the child wasn't building a sandcastle at all – but that she, the adult, assumed that was what she was doing, and therefore that she was failing. If we look at children from the height of the little hill we have captured, they are bound to seem unsuccessful adults. Unfortunately we have the power to act on our arrogant and mistaken assessment of the situation, and generally do so.

So we hurry on, desperately trying to organize the chaos that is building up in our own untranquil mind, listening only to what the child would mean if he were adult and not to what the child is saying.

I was once sitting in the garden at Neill's Summerhill, and a little girl of four or five came up to me, and asked what time it was. 'It's nearly twenty-five past three,' I said. She still stood there. A few seconds later she said, 'What time is it?' Somewhat surprised, I repeated my answer. Still she stood there, and a few seconds later she asked me again. 'But I told you,' I said gently. 'It's nearly twenty-five past three.' 'But what time *is* it?' she said.

The penny dropped. Her sweet patience and persistence, had far more guts than mine. I said humbly: 'It's twenty-three and a half minutes past three,' and she smiled and went away.

I've just met Mark. Brenda, who lives near by – aged four like Mark – was at the table. She had been 'invited'. Mark, already angry for private reasons, was indignant even to see her.

She placidly took a cake. 'If you take that cake, I won't like you!' She bit it. 'If you take that cake, I won't let you come in my house!' She took another bite and beamed. 'If you take that cake, I won't let you sit in my chair!' She took another bite. 'If you take that cake, I – I – I'll –!' then in a more resigned but still intense tone, 'Greedy guts.' She gave him a ravishing smile and said calmly 'I'm not a greedy guts' . . . and went on eating.

She ate up all the little cake while he stood watching, beside himself with rage. She took another, nibbled all the icing off, then put it back on the dish, smiling sweetly at Mark. In fury, Mark took all the little sweets off the top of the big cake. Brenda placidly picked up her spoon and pushed some green jelly round the plate. It melted as it circled. Mark watched with beetling brows – 'I don't like you!' Brenda, compliantly playing rather than retaliating, smiled happily and said, 'I don't like *you*' – and went on pushing the jelly. Mark scowled even more furiously.

He got under the table, and didn't actually kick her – his family is strong on good manners – but he made threatening kicking movements. Brenda, above the table, took no notice at all, just went on pushing the jelly. After a sizeable demonstration of menace, Mark very cautiously put his head up to see the results. Brenda, looking up from a spoonful, caught sight of him, and shrieked with laughter – a lovely relaxed earth-mother laugh – then seriously concentrated on the jelly again.

Puzzled, Mark withdrew under the table. He thought about it, then cautiously peeped out again. Same thing – a wonderful gurgling scream of laughter. Mark frowned, menaced, and shot down again. Once more he peeped up. And again that laughter. Now dawning on his face was the realization that the laughter was *for* him. His anger became pride, then delight. And he began to pop up and down, up and down, up and down. Brenda became completely hysterical with laughter and almost fell off her chair.

Mark, exhausted, rested for a moment under the table, then put his fingertips over the edge to pull himself up again. Brenda leaned over and tickled his fingers. Instantly Mark took umbrage – 'You scratched me!' Brenda was calmly eating jelly again, unconcerned. His mother had just come in and said in her quiet way, 'No, she tickled you.' 'Did she? Oh.' He thought about it.

At that moment his two boy friends came marching in with packets of sweets. He scrambled out, and they gave him some. 'Give some to Brenda!' he commanded.

'Who's Brenda?'

'My friend,' he said in a lordly way, putting his arm round her.

She lifted her face from her plate of jelly to give them her beautiful smile, took a sweet and got on with the jelly again.

I sat outside a 'one o'clock club' in a London play-park, and watched a small girl of about three grab a hefty wooden pram and start pushing it over the bumpy grass, concentrating hard. Eventually, yanking, thrusting, forcing it over the threshold, she managed to push it inside the inner area of a small climbing-frame that other children were playing on; there somehow she managed the even more difficult feat of turning it round, thrusting, yanking, forcing it out again. As soon as it was out – plonk! a larger black girl was seated in it. The two stared at each other, the first amazed, the second bold. At such a time you can almost hear children growing; they tick like small clocks. Just as time was moving towards some momentous resolution, a mother hurtled into the situation – 'Get out of it, will you!' – and dragged the second child out of the pram and righteously pushed the first on her way.

I consoled myself. In one o'clock clubs lonely mothers meet other lonely mothers and then turn their backs on their children. The situation would be played out again – without interference.

Five minutes later I saw the child again, sloped at 45° to the grass, head down, a larger child in her pram. In desperate spurts, then in a gradually accelerating conquering trot, she pushed the pram over the grass to the far end, then turned it. As she began to push it back, the larger child suddenly leapt out and ran off to some other game, and she continued her serious trundling alone. Neither of them had spoken. Each had carried out her own movement incommoded by the other's. Neither had stopped for the other. Neither had come to grief.

Muscles had been used, apprehension had dissolved, an undemanding temporary relationship had been made; a child had grown a little. And the mother, having made a friend, had not come between.

This is what nursery schools are for. They are not for aiming at
the A stream, for learning politeness and conforming to adults'
demands. They are a place where the child can *live exploringly* – in
his own rhythm, undisturbed by anxious adults.

My favourite state nursery school in this part of the country
is in a tough working-class area. It is not one of those trendy
easy-to-supervise places, built with the head and not the heart,
where every child can be seen at a glance from the head's glass
office and there are no private worlds. It is a large old house. The
children clamber of their own accord up the stairs, go into a room
and close the door and play in privacy if they want to. People have
said, 'But isn't this dangerous?' Yet there has never been an
accident. The kitchen is the warm scented heart of the place, and
the cook is chosen for the solace and mothering she offers, not
only for good cooking. (Indeed the meal-place and the lavatory
are places where young children ask their most important

questions and older ones hold many of their most important conversations. Yet they are the two specific places where orthodox teachers recoil from duty.) Two large trees grow in the garden – the Council originally sent men to cut them down, but the head stopped them, saying the children would need them. The days are filled with music and painting, and when you sit in the head's study the ceiling booms and thunders with the jumping dancing feet overhead, and little girls gravely set a picnic for themselves on the carpet, and from behind the settee on which you are sitting comes the rustle of a little boy, hidden, looking at books.

In this nursery school a new mother is encouraged, and helped, to sit still. I have watched so many new mothers in other nursery schools, wandering round with the child, making bright, too-bright conversations, showing him this, exclaiming at that, putting pressure without consciously meaning to, anxious to reach as quickly as possible the approved goal of child-settled-in-school. Here, a mother sits still and tranquilly waits. She takes out knitting, or looks at a magazine, a quiet base. The child clings at first to her lap, casting looks which perhaps he does not want to feel are noted, at the other children. And after a while, in little sallies of his own choosing, he begins to move out. Other children draw him. Music draws him. Stories being read draw him. Always he casts a glance back to the mother still sitting there, still quiet and unalarmed . . . until, of his own choice and in his own time, and of his own finding, he has become involved in a new creative community.

Of course, not all my local nursery schools are like that one. I read about one in the local paper, where a kind elderly couple had made a wendy house for the children. The paper said that the children were so pleased with it, that the kind couple said they were going to 'make another one for the boys'! I turned from this disconcerting text to an equally disconcerting photograph, where the little girls with neat bows in their hair and frilly dresses peeped coyly out of the doors of the wendy house, and leaned waving out of the windows; and it looked like nothing so much as a brothel.

Lea has just started at primary school.

She is lively, intelligent, talkative and sociable. 'Did you like school?' I asked her. 'Yes, it was lovely.' 'What did you like best?' . . . The new teaching methods? The paintings on the walls? The story writing? The young teacher? 'What I liked best was . . . two lovely juniors. They're called Martin and Terry. They came in our playground.' 'Is that allowed?' 'No. And Martin gave me a bottle of perfume.'

'What did he say?'

'He said, "It's for you."'

'And what did you say?'

'I said, "Is it really! I can't believe it!"' . . . I like Martin best, but they're *both* lovely.' She went on drawing a picture. 'That's what was best.'

6

Lea, at four, cut some clown shapes and ghost shapes out of white paper (she had been to the circus). She spread them carefully on the dark floor, and now there were dark clown shapes and white clown shapes and dark ghost shapes and white ghost shapes. Her father picked up one of the numerous instruments he plays and wanted Lea to sing a song he had written. Lea refused. Instead – for though put out he went on playing – she began to dance, and as she danced, from time to time without pausing in her movement she bent and picked up a ghost or a clown, and holding it in both hands at arm's length turned round in a circle, then laid it down again and continued gravely dancing. Her movement was completely natural, unforced from without or within, for quite serenely she had refused manipulation.

A year later I saw a leaf floating gently down a wide stream in Norfolk. Every now and then it turned round in a circle, then continued downstream. The same movement.

Yet if you were to say to a child 'Be a leaf floating downstream' you would be stupid. The child is far ahead of your adult artificiality.

This natural rhythm of children spreads out from the child, involving everyone, yet always remaining quite free, accepting other's freedom. It is not a physical exercise ; it is the rhythm of life.

Sometimes a child will be afraid, needing to know that the step forward will not wipe out the steps behind (like the new child in the nursery school who needs to know his mother is unalarmed by his step forward).

Julie, an enchanting and passionate child, suddenly went into one of her storms of panic and fury as she got ready to go to my nursery group. When her mother could penetrate her screams she said, 'What is it, darling ? If you don't want to go to nursery school, we won't go today.'

Instantly the screams were wilder. 'I *do* want to go !'

'Then I don't understand, darling. Why are you crying, then ?'

Frantic screaming, and eventually, 'Because I *like* being at nursery school !'

'Then why are you crying?'

'But I like being at home!' Frenzied screaming.

'Well, that's all right.'

'But I like being at nursery school!'

'Well, that's lovely for you, darling, having two things you like.'

Julie was lucky to have such a mature intelligent mother. With swollen-eyed radiance, Julie came on to nursery school, where daily she pursued her love affair with Stevie, also aged three. Julie loved many people passionately, her father, her teenage brother Alan as well. Summer came, and the first time she saw Stevie in the nursery garden with no clothes on she exclaimed with tremendous lingering pride for him, both maternal and loverlike, 'Oh, *Stevie*! You've got one of those things that Alan's got! You are lucky!' There was a charming out-going generosity about that remark that the Julie who first came to the nursery school – younger, tight and passionate – would never have shown. She liked to join the things she loved as she progressed. 'Dear Stevie,' she asked me to write one day, 'you are my friend. And you are Alan's friend.'

A child's rhythm, still unattacked, has a remarkably unegocentric, unselfconscious quality; even a suburban child can still be part of the universe, hearing and responding to its voices in a way the adult is not.

Innes Pierce and Lucy Crocker wrote in *The Peckham Experiment* of the appreciation that an anxiety-free child has of 'the total situation'. Anyone watching adults hurrying in different directions down a passage-way and children doing the same, the latter with no difficulty whatever, the former anxiously pulling up, desperately dodging, and finally taking deliberate decisions, will see what egocentric anxiety does to 'awareness of the total situation'.

Today, a father who had taken a trampoline to his small daughter's playgroup said to me, 'I thought they'd all fight for it – or all queue up for it; but they don't do either. There's always just the right number of children on the trampoline.' I'm sure he's never read *The Peckham Experiment*.

7

At the time I ran the nursery group, we had an Old English sheepdog. The first time I let him into the garden, the children were amazed. 'What is it?' 'It's a bear!' 'It's a pussy!' 'It's a bunny!' 'It's a lion!' (at this last, everyone ran away in a small flurry and came back half a minute later). 'What is it?'

Now I spoke for the first time. Complacently.

'It's a dog,' I said.

All hell broke loose. Tom hurled himself at me as if he were fighting for his life. 'It's not a dog! It's not a dog!' he screamed, fists and feet pulverizing me.*

In the middle of saving myself and comforting him, I wondered how any two year old comes to learn that alsatians, pekinese, collies, great danes, chihuahuas, are all dogs – are they all dogs because of what they do? (Then how can a twelve month old, used to a warm, furry, purring kitten, with twitching tail, lapping tongue and sudden, wild movements, recognize a cold, flat, shiny, silent and motionless picture in a book and name it 'pussy'?)

Once accepted as a dog and no longer threatening chaos, encouraged to take his verbal place calmly – a tiger sitting on a stool – in their growing classification, the bobtail was painted with vermilion splashes on one side, and was ridden on by Julian who was very light and lithe for his two years.

One day I put the dog's favourite toy – a medicine ball which he used to pretend to fight – in the garden just before the children arrived. Jonathan, aged four, saw it in the grass, rushed towards it, and drew back his leg to give it an enormous kick. It was evident he'd never seen a medicine ball before, so I quickly interposed my hand between the ball and his foot, not wanting him to break an ankle, and showed him its weight and resistance. He was disconcerted and surprised, and a little humiliated. So to restore his self-respect with facts, I said, 'It's called a medicine ball.' He poked it about with his hands, pushed it and pummelled it, exploring its possibilities, finding it hard work, still a little humiliated. Then –

* I used this true incident in more detail in a children's book *My Dog Sunday* (Hamish Hamilton).

'Why is it called a medicine ball?' he said.

I had never thought of this before. With an automatic move to keep my place in the hierarchy, even flippantly, I said quickly, 'Because it makes you strong, I suppose.'

He pushed it about a bit more, doubtfully. Then he said, 'Did you say it makes you strong?' 'Yes.' 'Well, it makes me weak.'

This is worth thinking about.

Many adults will render remarks like these harmless by laughing and repeating the story to other adults in front of the child, thereby turning the child into a clown and making it unnecessary for the adult to grow. Delight is very different from ridicule; one can laugh, but also one can learn. A child, candidly making a remark like this, taps a kaleidoscope and suddenly a new pattern forms, revealing not only the child, not only the world the child is describing, but ourselves; and if we are open to it we are lost in wonder and reappraisal. We hadn't realized before that we were bluffing, that we used clichés to keep our footing, or that we had betrayed our known experience for some academic abstract mumbo-jumbo like righteousness or vitamins (vitamins is an abstract mumbo-jumbo to 95 per cent of the people who religiously refer to them).

A three year old was sitting with her mother in a tube train opposite me. She pointed to an advertisement which must have been above my head and said to her mother, 'What is that Mummy pouring into that cup?' I twisted round to see. The advertisement was one for Cockburn's Port. All that the picture showed was two sets of fingertips, one set holding a glass, the other set pouring out. An adult would have assumed the fingertips belonged to a man; she assumed they belonged to a mother.

I looked hard at the advertisement after the two had got off, trying to see how far the adult assumption was rational. I thought, doubtfully, that *perhaps* the fingertips were masculine in shape (square and strong-looking), or *perhaps* the grip was masculine. But one makes the assumption, either the adult one or the child's, instantaneously – the adult probably influenced mainly by being able to read and knowing the social place of 'Port', the child making the assumption solely on the basis of experience.

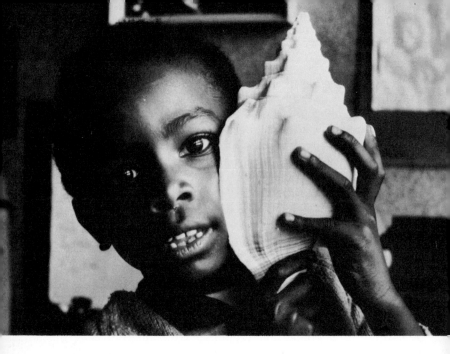

I heard of a child who played all day inseparably with a boy called Johnny, a West Indian boy. Johnny's mother went to work and Mandy's didn't, so Johnny had his meals with Mandy and went home at night. When Mandy and Johnny were five they started school. Mandy came home – without Johnny.

'Where's Johnny, then?' said her mother.

A haughty shrug. Silence.

'Where is he?'

Silence.

'Is he coming later?'

Silence.

The mother, perplexed, left her and went inside to get tea ready. Then –

'Tea's ready. Has Johnny come?'

Silence.

'Isn't he having tea today?'

Silence.

'What's the matter? Where *is* Johnny? Have you had a quarrel? What's happened?'

'Well!' said Mandy, tossing her head with what Blake called Experience. 'He never told me he was black!'

8

When I was a child in Salford and spring came to our street, bringing its breezes that blew jagged dust into streaming eyes and sent cabbage leaves bowling and floppeting awkwardly like crabs across pavements, and its sunshine that winked on the magic rainbows that your petrol-wet shoe made in puddles, then from far and wide – Cheetham, Strangeways and Lower Broughton – the children marched on our street, Fenney Street.

Home-made pockets full of nuts thumping against thighs, shoeboxes tucked under arms, boys and girls streamed into our street. Everyone had shoes on; for these games had pride in them, and those who took turns in shoes, and whose turn came tomorrow, waited at home.

Round the corner where Catholics and Protestants threw bewildering accusations at us ('Why did you kill Jesus?' 'Why do you drink babies' blood?'), springtime was Easter, with new straw hats and ribbons. But in our street, springtime was Passover.

For a whole week our pavements were smothered in children, crouching, crawling, crooning and shouting, in the Passover hazelnut games. There was the game you played over the hollows. You cradled the nuts in your palm, you whispered to them, prayed to them, begged and pleaded and bargained with them – sometimes in Yiddish, sometimes in English – then tossed them irrevocably, with a terrified regret for safety lost, into the little hollow. Some bounced out again with a brash, cheeky crack. Some went wide and rapidly rolled away, imprisoned swiftly again by the cracks between the flags. But some stayed in, rolling sweetly round, and shimmering into stillness at the bottom. They were the ones who won for you, did their best for you, your faithful friends. If you had more such faithful friends than the other players, you took the lot.

The other game for the proletariat was 'cupky', where you balanced four nuts – three points together and a nut on top – and the other children rolled their nuts to knock yours down. You took the nuts that went wide. A winner took all your four.

This was a game for little children, not old and tough and cunning enough to know the powerful magic that was whispered over the hollows, and not skilful, masterful and organized enough to have acquired an empty shoebox for the game of the élite who would undoubtedly get scholarships and become teachers and doctors and lawyers.

For this game you made holes in the lid, and wrote numbers above them. The smallest numbers – one and nought – went in the middle, where the cardboard, particularly as the week moved on, sagged invitingly. Three and four went near the corners that stayed high, proud and immune all week. Twos were scattered. Children hurled their nuts, with skill or just with zest, while you stood by your stall, hauling them in.

The wonderful thing about these games was that everybody won. At the end of each evening, no one was in tears; it was a time of unalloyed triumph. It must have had something to do with the bowls heaped high with nuts that stood in everyone's parlour, rich, generous and unaccounting.

And the rest of the year, when the outside world, the welcome callers-in, went back to Cheetham and Strangeways and Lower Broughton, the street remained ours. It was never empty. It belonged to us. The dirt cracks between the flags that we poked loose with a stick when we planted an apple pip, waiting for the mighty tree to grow overnight and burst the flags asunder; the bits of broken stick that we tied string round to make whips for our top, or sent sailing down the gutter and, flick, down the grid, while we whooped joyously alongside; the secret disturbing heart-clutching messages scratched at eye-level, 'Follow this line' (and you followed it compulsively, hoping that no one saw your weakness, till you came to the pay-off, 'Issy loves Zelda' or 'F—the Reds'); the wet glorying marks on the wall where two or three boys were arrogantly urinating, watched enviously, bitterly and with haughty head-tossing by physically-limited little girls (oh that glittering rainbow curve, the sheer height of it!); the high wall where you could bounce a ball, or build up a twisting chain of children playing 'The Big Ship sails through the Alley-alley-o', or the sad uncompromising file of 'Wallflowers, wallflowers, growing up so high, all you pretty flowers will soon have to die'; the lamp-posts where we tied frayed ropes and swung round, feet flailing; the wickets white-chalked on the walls; the hopscotch white-chalked on the pavement; and the Renoir smudges of coloured chalk that we spendthrifts trod on, and daubed and echoed recklessly among the cabbage-leaves – cyclamen, lemon and cornflower blue – all these were our marks, in our land.

The scissor-man with his sparking wheel, the rag-and-bone
man with his donkey and balloons, the Italian ice-cream man with
his massive feathery-footed horse and his fairground canopy,
the milkman with his churns and jugs, all these adults were our
friends who visited us in our territory. We watched them work,
worked with them, jumped on the back of their cart as they left
our territory and saw them off a little way, then slithered off,
bums and shoes scraping, and returned to our land.

There was fear in our streets too. I still remember an enormous drunk woman reeling lustily along full of terrifying good cheer. Just about held upright by a smaller sheepish friend, she bawled out her happy song. And behind her, flanked by two more enormous women, followed her little girl screaming in terror. I understood those screams. My ears still cringe with them. My spine still crawls. And I still see that child whose hard, familiar mother had become so strangely genial, possessed by such an alienly benevolent spirit.

And I was frightened too by the one flower I ever saw in our whole district, a huge insolent bully of a sunflower, who leered and jeered at me over a fence from a Bury New Road backyard. I always crossed to the other side of the road. Fear can come in all guises, laughing loudly or shaking a huge golden head, as long as it is strange.

There was hostility in our street too, Catholic against Protestant, Gentile against Jew, Conservative against Liberal, and both against Labour. The children were the infantry in these battles. We none of us ever knew what it was about; we were just loyal. Insults and stones were hurled, hair was savagely pulled. Children were made wretched and bewildered and bitter sometimes for the rest of their lives. But there was no personal animosity in it, no private decision; it was tribal. The most familiar song that was not a street game

Oh, the Blues, the jolly, jolly Blues.
The Blues shall live for ever.
The Reds shall die
With a carrot in their eye,
And the Blues shall live for ever!

was sung with a temporarily controlled violence that set the nerves leaping, a war-chant taken for granted.

And in the evening, in those warm spring and summer evenings (who says the climate has not changed?), the grown-ups would sit outside, some on the doorsteps joining their children who were sitting there already eating 'butties' with only a cotton shift on, and their bare bottoms terrifyingly vulnerable to their mothers' massive hands; and some, more genteelly, on bentwood chairs. And all inclined their heads graciously to their neighbours, and gossiped softly or shouted across the street till the lamplighter came.

Our street was full of drama. We lived in it. It was our territory. Every stage of our growth was marked on it, our wonderment, our terror, our triumphs, our deprivations, our compensations, our hate and our love. We knew every single person in our street. When, later on, I met rich people, and heard them talk casually but with such a sure love of 'our' river and 'our' woods, 'our' lake and 'our' fields, I was shaken. But I had forgotten 'our street', where, however squalid, grimy, violent, we too had territory.

For in the meantime I had become dispossessed. All of us, all the millions who never had woods or fields but had the street, have been dispossessed. And now I live in a London where people flee desperately from the clamour of unbearable crowds into the echo of unbearable loneliness, where pavements are not for playing children but for supermarket shoppers on the march, where the roads are smooth-surfaced for lethal cars, not cobbled for the huge mild horse of the rag and bone man, and where anything, however unimaginative, vindictive or half-witted, can be excused and even praised if only it 'keeps youth off the streets'.

For indeed there is always something disturbing, something that delicately fingers the spinal cord, something potentially menacing, about people who suddenly begin to do what they should have done in their early childhood. Our teenagers today have never owned their streets. When they stand at street corners they look dangerous. They may be plotting to take back what should have been their own. Drive them off. Mow them down. Enclose them.

9

In the 1890s in the Preface to her collection of *Children's Singing Games*, Alice Gomme wrote:

When one considers the conditions under which child-life exists in the courts of London (with which I am most acquainted), and of other great cities, it is almost impossible to estimate too highly the influence which these games have for good on town-bred populations. By watching slum children playing in them our reformers may learn a lesson, and perhaps see a way out of the dismal forebodings of what is to happen when the bulk of our population have deserted the country for the towns.

She did not foresee that when the bulk of our population had done just that, there would be no room for singing games in the streets.

The London streets have been closed to children for a long time now. They are merely paths, covered in haste and weariness, to and from the supermarket or the launderette. Where can a child put down roots and grow?

They live in flats – new flats – where their mothers keep all windows permanently locked because the child might fall; where the doors to the balconies – their only near-by playing space – are also kept permanently locked for the same reason; where the walls and floors are so thin that the children cannot even run across the room to hug their father when he comes home from work without neighbours complaining; where mothers walk round and round the block with the baby in the pram and the small children hanging on to the pram handle because the father, who is working nights, is sleeping; where the children who cannot play upstairs cannot play downstairs either, because the mother lives ten or twelve storeys up, and cannot see them or rescue them, and dangerous traffic threatens constantly.

The mothers themselves, packed in their hundreds in these up-ended shoeboxes, rarely see each other, rarely speak to each other. Up and down they go in the lift – if it works – silently.

Perhaps it is the inhuman 'loading' of them into these moving boxes, shoulder to shoulder, chest to back, that prevents them from speaking to each other. Perhaps it is because the lift is moving, and they are *being* moved, and at the end of this brief move they will separate again. Perhaps it is because this coming together in a lift is so uncasual, almost has the air of being arranged by authority. Anyway, they don't talk. You can get in the lift and an elderly woman may push in a man so drunk she props him against the wall where he sags, deaf and indifferent, as she hurls abuse, and punches hopelessly at him. 'Same every bleeding day! Fuck you, you bleeding fucking piss-hole!' simultaneously disassociating herself and expressing responsibility, angry and resigned and putting on an act for the one stranger. But no one else in the lift will say a word. They are like cart-horses so well trained they no longer have to wear blinkers.

When one day the lift breaks down, they trudge up a hundred stairs with their shopping and their pushchairs and their washing and their children, backs, arms, legs, tempers breaking; but on the stairs they meet people, individual people, and they take up their own chosen distance, and they linger, talking in pleasantly shocked tones about the 'disaster' that is secretly so welcome, becoming partly human again, until the machinery is mended and takes over once more.

And every weekend they go back to the crumbling street they were 'cleared' from – where their mother and father still live, where their old friends still lay mattresses on the floor to sleep on because beds would go straight through the floor boards, and the children who are left still roll marbles down the sloping floor, and the shopkeepers who have known them since childhood are still chalking things up; but soon, of course, everyone will be dispersed, into newer more hygienic buildings, and the exiles will have no old country to run home to, and will have their backs to the new white wall.

And people will get lost in the new white subways and the new white flights of steps, the drawing-board made concrete – until they learn to ignore their own senses, their own reason, their own memory, and meekly follow the notices, going the way they are told.

In their new flats, only a common enemy ever fills their dying loneliness and makes them feel alive. Only some menace – sometimes a fancied one – forces them to knock on each other's doors, and form alliances that have a faint bizarre resemblance to friendship. In this way, talk of 'a coloured family' moving in may get them drinking cups of tea in each other's flats, believing they are necessary to each other, believing they can act to shape their future, believing they can instead have their mother or their daughter living near them. Then a local paper gleefully publicizes their sad little petition, and wild threatening notes are pushed through their letter-boxes; door-chains are bought and panic joins loneliness. And on the huge wall behind the busy modern police station, fascist slogans will be white-washed at night.

And all that time, you will probably find, no one has ever seen this 'coloured family', and never will. Did they exist? Or were they a sick joke, like a paper bag burst by some fool to waken a pathetic confused old man and set him leaping?

But the children, who for a brief time were responsible messengers for parents who suddenly acquired vitality and power and importance and solicitude, will go to their school and say, 'The blacks take our homes.'

But sometimes their flats are old ones. Some friends of ours, a few years ago, made a short film round one of these blocks . . . the windows blanked with squares of cardboard, like cornplaster, the idiotic gibbering archway standing pompously in the gap of a tumbled wall, the brick-littered, old-iron-piled dump where children play (digging holes in the ground with hunks of twisted iron, scooping loose dirt in jagged tin cans, and on occasion casually, amiably and tentatively tossing bricks at each other – children in all respect like the children of my Salford childhood,

except that these children are well dressed). And beyond, line after line spanning the cleaving alley, stretch those ropes of babies' nappies, so astonishingly white, that have not been in Southwark long enough to turn grey. I remember I had almost accepted the place as a film-set, and suddenly it froze my blood to see a postman with a bag of letters trudging up inside the iron grilles they call staircase windows here, and to realize that people lived there, wrote and received letters behind those iron bars.

The children flocked round. First six, soon close on a hundred. 'Is it for telly?' they wanted to know. A little girl who looked about eight pulled a packet of Woodbines from her pocket. 'Want me to smoke?' she said obligingly. They were very cooperative and knowledgeable. 'Get out of the way!' they shouted. 'He's the shooter!' They enjoyed the word 'shoot' – enjoyed the chance to use it in a new context, an approved prestigious context, and they used it with wit. 'Don't move or they'll shoot you!' they shouted, and yelled with laughter.

The adults instantly thought the film was being made to remedy the housing, done for their benefit. Like besieged people, they welcomed the liberators . . . but coolly. ' 'Bout time too,' said one woman sternly. 'Should have made a film here years ago. Might get something done now.'

'Is it a documentary?' said one elderly man. 'Is it about *the conditions*?' My inside turned over when he said that. Not 'Is it about what we've got to put up with?' but 'Is it about *the conditions*?' an approved, alienated, expert, sociological word. Over and over again, you meet this in these hopeless districts. People have lost their own inner drive; they see themselves as things experts are interested in. Anyone with an educated accent is seen at once as a representative of the mysterious People with Power – the Council, the Telly – who must be seized and bombarded with demands. Any protest that you are not from 'Authority' turns you into an enemy, withholding things from them, not just a bastard but a cunning bastard.

I remember how a woman said with a certain self-preening – confidentially staking a claim to high standards – 'Took us months to get them to pull down the rubbish-heap there. Got as high as *that*' – she indicated a fantastic height, like a mountain – 'over-run with rats, it was. The landlord took out the chutes, see, and the people started to chuck the rubbish out of the window. Foreigners, you know. Don't know any better.' And then a lorry-driver put his head out of the window as he went by, and shouted 'They don't want to film it, mate. They want to blow it up!'

Well, they didn't blow it up. But they cleared the jagged-iron-strewn dump where the children played – and turned it into a *car park*. Where do the children play now, in their gay, good clothes?

If they don't live in flats, they still live in the old tenement
terraces that literally fall down around them – specially the large
families, the final rejects, for the councils are building new
accommodation only for the small families who can be neatly
packed into these boxes-in-boxes like uniform wedges of frozen
fish in a refrigerator. And here the children can only play on the
dark broken stairs, or in the one usable room where everything
takes place, and where their night is always light and their day is
always twilight, and where the stove wreathed with steam rising
from boiling water, boiling washing, boiling fat, dominates the
room like Moloch. Often, the trapped mothers fasten the
children, even the four year olds, into cots or high chairs or prams
where they cannot move, and tight-lipped and deeply depressed
refuse to speak to them or touch them except in sudden anger.
They come to school at five, scarcely able to walk or talk. Such
children look listlessly at dolls and cots and all the warm
paraphernalia with which other children play out family life.
But once I saw two older ones, seven and eight, find the wendy
house. They began to play with it, pretending to be a mother and
child in a kitchen, cooking – not lovingly but with nightmare
anxiety! At least it was good that they could at last play out the
nightmares.

I saw a television documentary recently that filmed an area like this, and showed the high spot of the children's school holiday – the time when other children went to the country, to the sea – when into these harsh, crammed, noisy streets a bulldozer arrived to demolish some of the buildings, and the dust was ten times thicker than usual, and the usual jangling row was raised to shattering mind-blasting pitch, and the children were excited and thrilled to become absorbed in the world's work, and to watch *official* destruction. It was only demolition work that they ever saw – no quiet building.

In Islington, a London borough with 11,000 on the housing list where twenty-two acres is taken up by prisons, a deputation went to the Home Office because the Government had announced that it was going to rebuild one of the prisons, Holloway. The leader of the deputation asked, 'Would there be any open space left over when Holloway is rebuilt? . . . There is nowhere for a mother to go with a pram, even for a walk.' But the Minister of State for Home Affairs (a sardonic title in the circumstances) said that if there were any open space left they would build another prison there.

At the opposite end of London, my end, I went to visit a sick man's family. When I came into the living-room where he lay, I saw that his bed had been moved, from the best wall whose only fault was that the draughts whistled through the holes behind the wallpaper, to a wall so sodden the paper peeled off at a touch like bark from a tree. This wall was under the window. It was summertime, and he wanted to see out into the garden. The garden! A strip of yard where the only tap was, and where the children kicked the lavatory door before they went in to drive off the rats.

Mr King stretched out a little, and rested his elbow on the broken window-sill under the broken sash-cord. A rat actually jumped there, paused a moment and stared at him. Mr King joked chirpily, 'A rat may look at a King!' Rats didn't seem to worry him except that he didn't like the children having to drive them out of the lavatory. (But perhaps they would worry him more, I thought, if he were not dying?)

He had recently acquired some friends, reliable friends who have initiative, and knowledge of how the world is run – the NSPCC. When I called, the NSPCC Inspector had managed to get paint and wallpaper. But she couldn't use them when the walls were so wet, so she had got on to the Sanitary Department of the Borough Council, hoping they might chase the landlord. But the landlord wants them out; then he'll do up the cottage and let it for four times the rent. In fact, he offered them £150 to go. Mrs King, a simple soul, was enchanted and thought it very kind of him, but Mr King and the Inspector thought otherwise. How would a dying man and his inadequate wife and the four children still at home find anywhere else to live? Meanwhile the walls drip and the rats scamper and the plaster falls in a flurry from holes in the ceiling; and we wondered what would happen if instead the Sanitary Department condemned the house – what a desperate chance to have to take.

Upstairs, though, one of the two rooms is drier. This is the one
where the floor has a huge hole in it, and slants so much you can
scarcely stand upright. Another Inspector and the eldest boy
painted it last weekend, and now the three youngest sleep there in
the gaiety.

From his bed, Mr King, responsible and capable, ran family
affairs. He gave his wife money to buy a loaf of bread, and
received back the change, counting each penny, when she
returned, for she is not very bright. She talks of his 'running sores'
with the same scatter-brained interest as she might of her
daughter's wedding-cake, and wonders chattily why he cries
sometimes.

I got up to go. And then suddenly, he said something that was
startling coming from him, a practical man concerned, even when
he is dying, with payments on time, with rent tribunals, landlords,
public assistance and rat catchers and all the responsibility of
running a home. 'I wish you could find out for me,' he said,
'where I could get a canary. A Yorkshire or a Norfolk or an
African canary. I used to breed them once, you know.' I was
shaken.

Going home I thought, was it hope, or an obstinate insistence on his right to a future, or is it just a need for limpid tranquillity at the end? And what would a canary swinging from that rotting window, where the fetid air from the gasometer meets the stench from a dying man, what would it make of the rats, and the rats of the canary? Wouldn't the canary's singing drench his end in a glorious shower of golden notes like fireworks in the evening, and make the children's eyes dance, and his simple, cheerful wife more cheerful and light-headed still?

And I thought, supposing one of the children managed to write about this in school ('My Pets' . . . 'my rat and my canary') in chaotic formations or explosions of words. Would the teacher give her good marks? Would she lovingly reciprocate? Or would it be 'in very bad taste'?

But some districts are 'better', more open, more sophisticated. Mine is one. Just up the road from me is another council block, a human-scale one. Someone had the bright idea of mixing young couples who had small children, with old people. So the Council built maisonettes with lower flats which they let to old people and upper flats which they let to young families. The children are not allowed to play in their flats, because the old people cannot stand the noise. They are not allowed to play on their balconies because the old people can't stand the noise. They are not allowed to play on the path because the old people might fall over them. And of course they are not allowed to play on the grass, the tidy mown cherished piece of grass, because not only can the old people not stand the noise, but the grass is sacred.

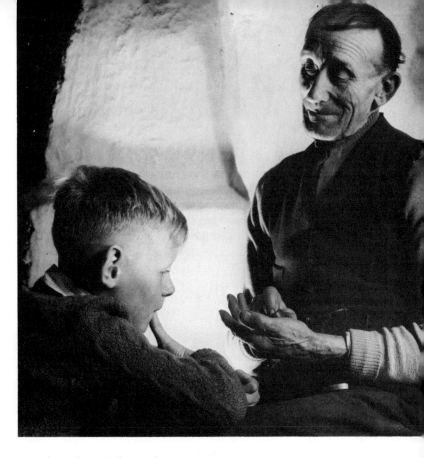

Jacky, a friend of mine from another street, once paused at the
notice board on a grassy overgrown triangle of land, and read out
'Children are not allowed to play on the grass'. Jacky being only
four, we said, 'Can you read then?' 'No,' said Jacky scornfully.
'Then how did you know it said that?' And surprised at our
ignorance, she matter-of-factly answered, 'Well, wherever's
there's grass, children aren't allowed to play on it, are they?'

Once when the Council had sent a man to mow the lawn in
front of the maisonettes, the scent of the cut grass in the sun got
into the children's noses and made them drunk, and they ran
about kicking the amazed stuff into the air, and picking it up in
cushiony handfuls to breathe its juicy sweetness, and rolling over
and over like cows on sunsoft windfalls or cats on catmint,
shrieking and laughing for joy. The caretaker said grimly he was
phoning for the Council and we'll see about that.

And another day, someone had given a small boy a huge bag of conkers. He took them outside, and other children came and sat on the path and he divided them between them all because there were so many. Some children had as many as ten each. They were very beautiful. 'The old people will fall on them,' shouted the caretaker, and 'We'll see about that', and phoned for the Council – or said he was going to.

So he builds up in these small children – because he himself cannot cope without these divisions – a hatred of the old people who could have been leisurely, placid, experienced companions for them, glad of the vitality and the renewed growth the children brought them. The children grow aggressive, and sullen and smouldering.

The tenants held a meeting. 'Can't the children have just a bit, just a narrow strip, that is their own to play on?' they said. No. 'Where can they play then, if they can't play in their flats, or on the balconies, the paths, the grass?' Outside in the street, he said. The street is the main London–Brighton highway. One child has already been killed there.

So, in this block of maisonettes, where the Council caretaker is ever alert for trespassers – children who live there and try to play – a mother rebelled. In hot summer, when a pink copper cloud hung in the sky tenuously dissolving, and in other parts of London the trees were lush and shady and the grass wide and welcoming and the white paths were bobbing with grave nursemaids and gay au-pairs and all the elegant fantasy of high prams with tasselled canopies, she bought a small plastic paddling pool. She put it in the middle of the holy patch of grass, and poured jugfuls of water in it. It was for everyone. The children came running.

The adults were aghast, frightened, unnerved. What would happen? What vengeance would be taken? The caretaker said he'd get the Council. The rebel mother said she didn't care if he did; by the time they arrived, the children's day would be over. He kept coming out and shouting he was phoning the Council; they were on their way, now, he shouted. Championed by this one mother, the children defied him. The Council never came. You could say the children had won. But the happiness had gone out of them. Until the caretaker had threatened them, they had been playing there naturally, because the sun was blazing down and it was natural to splash in cool water, crisscrossing the soles of your damp bare feet with grass and washing it off again in the rocking water. They had been splashing, shouting, revelling, absorbed in the cool caress of the water, watching with interest and curiosity the explosive splash, the startled spray, the single winking drops on a blade of grass. But then they stopped playing naturally. They were playing mock-furtively, defiantly, angrily, tauntingly, not in creative pleasure but in battle. They would run to the pool and dip a toe in, their head over their shoulder to hear a shout from the caretaker, the shout more exciting than the water whose pleasure was forgotten. They were no longer free. They were chained to the pool by the adult's enmity, all creativeness gone. Then one by one, they went indoors, not knowing why the glory of the sun that still shone had gone down for them – until only one or two were left, beginning to throw things sullenly, small things at first. Maybe soon the caretaker would have something bigger to phone the Council for.

10

London hates children. Children are the bottom of the pile, the lowest rung of the ladder, the small scapegoat available to the most inadequate or the most harassed adult. And London creates harassed adults, and, by its ever-increasing impossible demands, inadequate ones.

We have an appalling bus service here. When the children come out of school, and there is already a long line of people waiting at the bus stop, the adults become vicious. Hate moves along the line palpably stiffening everyone. 'Bloody little devils.' 'We had to walk when we were their age!' 'Taking grown-ups' seats!' 'Oughtn't to be allowed!' 'Bloody devils!' 'Why don't they make them walk!' The conductor cooperates by yelling at the children and ordering them off the bus whenever he can, thus winning passengers' friendship in a way that – the service being so maddening – only happens when they are both united against someone else.

When a young friend of mine moved up to secondary school and found himself having to take this bus, he was so upset by the grown-ups' anger that he preferred to walk – and it was a long way – however late he got home.

About that time, in a different district, a small girl was assaulted. She had been walking home from school, and a lot of accusations were made against her mother for being so mean as not to give her bus-fare; but the mother said that she did give her bus-fare, but the grown-ups were so nasty to the kids for getting on the buses that she said she'd sooner walk.

Yet further north, where the cities are smaller and you can see the hills at the end of the street, they are not nearly so hateful to children. I was on a bus in Sheffield when the schoolchildren came out, flooding to the bus stops. Now a Londoner, I cringed.

But nobody swore at the children. I could scarcely believe it. The kids hurled themselves on to the bus, clattered clumpily up the stairs, crowded into the downstairs – and the passengers *smiled* at one another in a loving family complicity, and the conductor joked with a horde of lads on the platform, pretending to punch them. It was amazing to me, and wonderful.

Two little schoolgirls in warm winter scarves sat near the conductor. Or rather, only one sat; the other one was leaning forward and then standing up and talking to the conductor, and the two of them, the child and the man, had this conversation in their slow unconstrained Sheffield voices that give everyone the same amount of respect:

'How old do you have to be, to be a conductor?'

'Well, I don't know. Let me think. . . . Eighteen. Yes, eighteen you have to be.'

'Eighteen . . .'

'Why did you ask? Do you want to be one then?'

'Yes.' (All this very slow and long-drawn-out.) 'I think I'd like to be a conductor. I like running up and down stairs, you see. . . . But I'm only ten. It's a long time to wait . . . I'd have to wait eight years. It's a long time, eight years. . . . But oh, I *do* want to be something!'

There was in her voice and in her face that awareness of gradually moving time, of time moving one along to some special moment unconjectured as yet but surely so wonderful when it comes. This is something you only see in girls.

You see it here in London in the faces of sixteen year olds, leaning against lamp-posts in their school uniform waiting for the bus, with their hair escaping in golden tendrils from useless school hats. You see it in the office girls, wakened from their dreams by the alarm clock yet still dreaming, hair still muzzy from the pillow, eyes still smudgy and cloudy from sleep, teetering up the High Road in stiletto heels, bandaged so tight in their short skirts, they *charleston* to get on the bus and the conductor has to haul them aboard in their ridiculous enchanting incapacity. Everything they do has this larger echoing touching quality; so that what they actually say is only a starting point for your surprised response to them. Somehow they are always potential. They are never completely in the present but always leaning forward. They have that extraordinary hopefulness that is always on the brink of turning into delight. They are waiting, but not for the bus. They have been clanged awake before full-time but not only by that cheap alarm clock. Yes, they *do* want to be something. But they don't know what it is.

This is something quite different from the adult-willed assertion, the aggression, even sometimes the edginess, of the boy who wants to be a bus conductor, or an engine driver, or an astronaut, or a physicist. But I have never seen this quality so clearly in a girl as young as ten.

So maybe it is no use grabbing them by the shoulder and yelling down their ear, 'You are a failure! I have proved it!' and 'You have failed again!' and 'There is no future for you, nothing for you at all!' Because they don't hear, they just smile sleepily but not at us, and our nagging, hostile, ignorant voices do not break into their dream.

But you know, you could never hear a conversation like that on a London bus.

Grass is not for playing on, flowers are not for picking, trees are not for climbing. In London, a child in a tree splits the sky asunder, thunder seems to crack, lightning forks, and any adult near thinks at once of Borstal.

I once passed an adventure playground where five or six boys of twelve or so were climbing some high ramshackle construction, so high that it was very visible above the fence – a mistake to be paid for, as all adventure playground workers know – when a man with a bowler hat and a neatly rolled umbrella came by. He stopped, horrified. He could scarcely believe his eyes. A policeman on the corner was leaning on the bonnet of a car, making notes. The man walked swiftly up and poked the policeman in the arse with his umbrella. 'Officer!' he said. 'Officer!' The policeman clenched his teeth and said nothing. The man poked him again. 'Officer! Officer!' A few more sharp pokes and commands, and the policeman, fuming, and still refusing to turn round, said 'Just what is the matter, sir?' 'Look!' – the man waved his umbrella; he was incoherent – 'Look!' 'Look at what?' said the policeman with deliberate weight. 'Those boys! Look! They're climbing!' 'They're allowed to, sir,' said the policeman. 'It's their playground.' 'But . . .!' 'If you don't mind, sir, I'm busy here.' 'But – they're climbing!' 'I know, sir. There is nothing I can do, sir.' 'But – they're climbing! It's fantastic! Disgraceful! Appalling!' The policeman presented only a wide impervious arse, so the man walked into the road, halted the traffic imperiously with a wave of his umbrella and marched over, exclaiming aloud, 'Fantastic! Disgraceful!' turning around as he crossed to wave his umbrella at the oblivious boys.

I have seen three city girls sent crazy-drunk in springtime by the unknown, unexpected sight and smell of unfenced Council-laid-out beds of tossing daffodils, so that they rushed at them and picked them and threw them all in the air, like an ecstatic puppy in one's arms will gobble up a bunch of violets, quite out of their senses – or maybe at last in them.

I have seen children in a park warned off from picking blossom, encouraged by a sympathetic adult to pick the dandelions that grew among the grass, thinking that was safe for them. But I saw the dandelions whipped away from them by an outraged keeper who scourged them with withering words, and then, before the children's agonized eyes, rammed the flowers into a rubbish bin, smashing them down righteously to make sure they could not be rescued or revived.

The children on Council estates cannot keep animals, and cannot grow flowers. I am sure children need to be in touch with the earth, need to have their fingers in soil, and their eyes looking into an animal's, or a bird's eyes. These children are dissociated from the universe, and the rhythm of the universe; they are like a note that has been hurled out of the score.

But in the city, rain is only an enemy. Earth is the horrid detested dirt that they furtively, guiltily, bring in on their shoes. Rain turns dirt to mud, and you get clobbered for that. The approved ground is concrete. What you grow things on is blotting paper.

Up the road from here is some parkland. And there I saw four children playing. Their ball went up into a tree. And suddenly, tumbling through the leaves an apple fell down. The children were wonder-struck. An apple falling out of a tree! How did it get up there?

They examined it to see if it was real, and were amazed that it was. Gravely, and a little troubled by the mystery, they began to play again, stealing sidelong glances more and more often at the magic tree until at last, semi-accidentally, the ball again sailed up into the tree, and wonder of wonders, another apple came down.

Now it was settled beyond any doubt! They were seized by glorious merriment, a wild delight, and over and over the ball shot up into the tree, and the apples pelted down, tiny, wormy, enchanted apples. And such enchanted children. Never in their lives had they seen such a thing – apples growing on trees, like a picture in a book!

The adult with them was entranced by their delight, and with the knowledge that came to them with the delight, a revelation; and she pretended she saw nothing whatever, just sat among the falling leaves and twigs and apples with an eye alert for a keeper. But soon her friend came up, good citizenship overriding all delight in her, and was shocked and stern and a little frightened. They went home. But the children took the magic apples with them hidden in their pockets, apples that grew on trees, imagine!

Someone once told me that when she was a child in Vienna her mother bought up one whole summer crop of a cherry tree for the children. For a spring, summer and autumn, the tree was the children's. Nose-deep in spring in the creamy curds of blossom, perched in summer in among the swinging cherries, mouth and clothes stained crimson with the season's culmination, they lived in their cherry tree. They were at one with the sky, an accepted part of the whole, wide, magical, reasonable, rhythmical world.

11

Children, because they are small and weak, because they have had little experience, and because it suits us to condition them quickly before they have more experience, become secretly convinced we are omnipotent, and that any catastrophe is the result of our wrath, our wrath with them. If the sky were to fall on them, they would think it had happened because they had peed on the floor when we had warned them not to.

What dreadful crime they have committed, that has made some children rejected and unloved, the children do not know. But after all, in most people's childhood, it is punishment that tells them they have committed a crime, and this has always been enough. So unloved children know, not that their parents are at fault, unhappy or inadequate, but that they – the children – have committed a crime.

There are some homes where these rejected children are kept at bay with cold meaningless gifts, or are reckoned up in terms of the examinations they pass, or are hatefully ignored so that they do not even know for sure that they are there, let alone when or how they committed their crime. These homes are called 'good' homes, so society says nothing to these children. Never openly accused, they spend their lives desperately hiding the 'knowledge' of their guilt, the secret 'knowledge' that they are murderers – they murdered love. Teachers like children like this. They work hard and pass examinations, because they know they are always on trial.

But in other homes, these children are beaten, or deliberately burnt, or left naked on soaked mattresses. And then society itself confirms with a clap of thunder their terrifying fantasies. Society itself surrounds them with policemen, takes them to court, tries them, and condemns them to be taken away from everyone they know and shut up in a special place where only other like criminals live. We call this place a Home.

I have seen children in these Homes. They sidle up to any stranger. They cling to you, they slide their hands inside your sleeves, they rub themselves against you – not in tranquil friendliness but in a grotesque masturbation, and not only that,

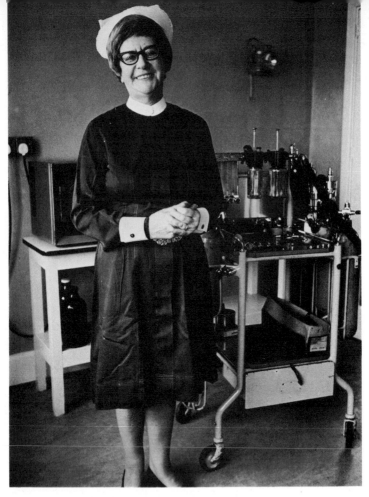

but almost as if they are trying to define themselves, to outline
themselves, to tell themselves, 'That is where I feel something;
that must be my surface.' And some visitors, getting out of their
cars and pausing for a minute to let the glow of doing a worthwhile
thing fall on them like sunshine, are flattered, actually flattered,
thinking this insistent wriggle of arms and legs is due to their own
personal charm. 'Aren't they sweet!' they exclaim, modestly
distracting attention from themselves. Sweet! My God, they are
obscene. They are not human. The essential attribute of a human
being, the physical identity they should have felt in babyhood,
the calm assurance of being loved and therefore of loving, has
been taken away from them. And far far behind everything they

do – growing only deeper as years and experience and fortuitous happenings are piled on top like earth on a corpse – is the bottomless despairing conviction that they have committed an unspeakable crime. It must indeed be unspeakable, since no one ever speaks of it.

I knew two children from a Home. Brother and sister, they had half-brothers and sisters scattered all over the country. Their Home was an estate separated by large gates from the ordinary world. They never nipped round to the shop on the corner, they never jumped on a bus, or greeted you in a park, or climbed trees for conkers in the gold of autumn and hidden in the leaves heard the conversation of strangers. They lived only among their kind. What was their kind? Well, these two were children who, ten years before, screamed beside their father as he hanged himself; their mother had abandoned them – gone off with another man. Their kind ran in this Home to four hundred or so.

But once every three weeks they were invited into the outside world by a friend of mine who for seven years, while the children were moved from place to place, and their files were lost, and the adults who dealt with them had changed over and over again, had remained their constant 'auntie'.

After all those years, they still marvelled at the things that went on in her house – that 'uncle' shaved, that he went to work every morning, that he and 'auntie' slept in the same bed, that they went to shops, chose what they wanted to buy and paid with money, that vegetables had names like 'cauliflower' and people ate them. . . . Her home was a strange and remarkable place, almost eccentric they would have thought if they had gained the vocabulary to think with. It was the only place where they could keep individual possessions – a toy, a jar of paint, a frilly petticoat, white knickers, a hair ribbon, a hamster.

It was in her house that I saw the case they had brought with them that weekend from the Home.

One blue jersey, ragged, unravelling, full of large holes. One dirty shirt, faded to grey, full of tiny holes. Two separate halves of pyjamas, the top half filthy, the bottom half clean, both the size for a child half this age, both so washed out they might almost have been the same pattern but they weren't. One filthy shirt, faded to two completely different colours. Everything was dirty and disintegrating, everything was several sizes too small. Everything had a name inside, some several names, and not one name their own. Yet my friend was constantly buying them clothes, clothes that they delighted in because they were like hers, or 'uncle's', or her own children's; but as soon as they got them Home they were 'lost', their housemother told them, and they never saw them again.

So in this way and in many many other ways, always coming between the two children and their 'auntie' and 'uncle', the authorities confirmed for the children what their first abandonment had already told them – not that any adults were at fault, but that they were not fit to be loved.

And when they are no longer children, neither the 'clever' child who has survived examinations, nor the 'dull' child from the Home, what becomes of them? How many of them can ever make a full relationship? How many of them dare? How many dare stand naked before another human being and say, 'I committed the crime of not being loved. Am I forgiven?'

Nina has been working for a fortnight in a one o'clock club. She wrote to me:

There is a very tough kid who comes here – Susan, her name is, and she's eight. She is brimming with confidence, and talks in a strident, capable, cockney voice: ''Allo, miss! You alright, miss? I'll 'elp you, miss!' She looks at you with her face tilted down slightly, and her eyes watchful and steady, as if she's ready for you to shout or hit out at her at any moment. She's not frightened or beaten – just defiant and strongly ready for any provocation into battle.

Today she came with her three older brothers – eleven, twelve and thirteen years old – except that one of them said she wasn't his sister but his girlfriend. They look extraordinarily alike, these two! This particular 'brother' came up to me:

'Are you "Miss"?'

'Yes' – laughing.

'No, you're not.'

'Well, I'm supposed to be.'

'You carrying things in? I'll do it.'

'Thanks very much. You could help me with this table.'

'No, *I'll* take it' – the same under-the-eyebrows way of looking at you, and never a flicker of a smile.

Then Susan, with her usual 'You alright, miss?', and the two other boys joined in carrying heavy equipment from the field to the hut.

Pauline saw them in the hut – officially a play area for under-fives only. 'Come on now – out you go, you older children – you're too big to be here.' My helpers ignored her. She banged on the table and yelled at them. They scooted. Just outside the hut, one of them grabbed a toy iron and ironing board and ran off with it, another knocked over some toys, and a third took a toy trolley and ran with it, dragging it over the fence with him. All four of them were very angry. So was I.

'They were helping,' I told Pauline.

'No, they weren't.' (How to cope with *that* one?)

'They *were* helping *me*,' I said, and went towards where the four kids were, calling '*Please*, come back!' They ignored me – understandably, I thought.

I carried on with my work. Pauline ran over to the fence shouting shrilly, 'Bring back those things at once, will you? Come on now, you *horrors*!' I went into the hut.

A few moments later Pauline came smugly in with the four kids. 'They're going to help us – *officially*.' 'Well, of course,' I said, 'they were helping before.' And I smiled at the kids. 'Thank you,' I said.

We finished carrying all the stuff inside and I stood on the step chatting to the four of them. Suddenly the thirteen year old bent down and picked something up from the sand by the step. 'I've found threepence,' he said, and then – conflict flashing across his face as he glanced at me – 'No, I 'aven't.' And he clutched the threepenny piece, looking confused and guilty. 'Finders keepers,' I said, smiling. There was no one around bewailing the loss of threepence. The lad stood up, thrust his hand out, ''ere you are.' I took the threepenny piece, and handed it back to him, saying, 'It's Friday – here's a weekend present for you.' And he took it. Immediately the twelve year old put his hand in his pocket and took out a penny (one he had found somewhere?) ''Ere you are, miss,' he said. I took the penny, laughed, and gave it back to the boy, saying, 'Happy Friday.' And he popped it back in his pocket.

After a bit the eleven year old said, 'You here Monday? See you Monday.' '*I* won't be here,' I said (today was my last day at the Play Park). 'Oh well, see you anyway. We'll come and help you.' 'Yes, we'll come and help,' they all said – no smiles, just facts. 'Smashing,' I said, and turned to go into the hut. 'Miss, miss!' from the eleven year old. I turned back. 'Yup?' I said casually. 'I want to give you something,' he said, and as I looked at him, I saw him let go of a handful of sand behind his back. 'Oh no!' I laughed, 'I don't want a load of sand in my face, thanks!' 'No,' he said, 'I want to whisper something.' I bent my head down. He kissed my cheek. 'Now me,' said the thirteen year old, and he kissed me on the cheek too. 'Your turn!' ordered the eleven year old to the twelve year old, who was a bit embarrassed and blushed. 'He doesn't have to if he doesn't want to,' I said, 'but thank you – you've *made* my weekend' – and I really meant it. I was very moved and pretty amazed.

The four kids turned and left – sturdy, grave, tough, rough bullies of kids – two of them to return to junior school on Monday, and two of them to a 'home' in a fortnight's time. 'Ta-ra,' they called as they climbed over the fence, still unsmiling. And on the other side they hurled themselves on top of one another in a rough tough-kids' fight.

12

I was talking about writing for children, and of children's need to work through grief, fear and catastrophe. And someone in the audience said she lived near Aberfan, where in October 1966 the coal tips engulfed a village and buried the school, wiping out almost a whole generation. Her boy, age seven, insisted that the television news be kept on all day long. The adults wanted to turn it off; they found it unbearable; but the child would not allow them to. For five days that child watched the television screen, the digging, the weeping, the floodlights, the carrying away of dead children, the coffins, the flowers. For five days he insisted on seeing the newspapers, the photographs, the headlines. The adults were near breaking-point, yet they managed to continue to trust the child.

During these five days, he began to play with his 'Action Man' toy, twisting the doll's limbs and body into contorted agonizing shapes, very disturbing to the adults. Then he began to make a pile of his toys in the middle of the room – still with the television set on. He got his torch and fixed it so that it shone on the huge heap. Then finally he set his Action Man on top of the heap and brought him crashing to the bottom. The parents were sick and full of dread. But the child was finished with it. He had come to terms.

He had been completely relaxed and able to take all difficulties in his stride ever since, said his mother. But many parents can't stand such exploration. They have had to suppress so much in themselves that a child's explorations terrify and agonize them, and they forbid them. But these parents let the child's natural rhythm have its way. How often does this happen?

In Leicester, recently, someone told me she had been talking to a child in school that morning, a girl of seven. The conversation went something like this.

I'm getting a pound on Friday, Miss.

Are you really? A pound of what? A pound of potatoes?

No! A pound of money!

Oh. What are you going to spend it on?

Not going to spend it. It's for my Grandad's funeral.

Has your Grandad died?

No. My *Gran's* died.

But you said it was for your *Grandad's* funeral.

Well, my Gran's died, and my Grandad's got to pay for the funeral. And he says he hasn't got the money. He's got to get seven or eight pounds. So my Dad says he'll give him a pound when he gets paid on Friday. And my Mum says she'll give him a pound when she gets paid on Thursday. And everyone's giving him a pound for Gran's funeral . . . So I'm giving him a pound for *his own* funeral.

There was so much expressed by this child. Love and consideration for her grandfather, who must have seemed to her to have only the worry and none of the kudos of this family event; perhaps she had a special reason for identifying with someone who got left out when the giving took place . . . the booking of a place in the capable adult world where you could give valued help to those you love . . . and, through this acceptance of a practical fact and practical action, a coming through grief.

But how many teachers in a city school, where they set up a middle-class bulwark against the working-class life that maybe was theirs, could accept such a fantasy, if fantasy it is, and enjoy such a story? How many teachers in any case can accept the fact of death? They come from a social group that tends to shut away disturbing things lest they become overwhelming. And being surrounded by children always moving past them and out into the world while they remain behind, there must often be with them, making a counterpoint with the perpetual youth the recurring waves of children bring them, a deep regret for time gone and an awareness of approaching death. Working-class life, and death – these are two things to keep battened down.

I told the story of Grandad's funeral at Wolverhampton, and a headmistress said that the previous day, at assembly, she became aware of a small girl, seven years old, rubbing against her.

'What is it, Valery?'

'My Auntie May died yesterday.'

'Oh I *am* sorry, love. Put it in your news' – patting the child, and moving on to something urgent.

A couple of hours later, there was Valery again, pressing against her.

'My Auntie May died yesterday.'

'Oh I *am* sorry, love' . . . and again having to move on.

This happened twice more during the day; and she said to herself, 'I really must get Valery to herself in my room, so that she can get it all off her chest, poor lamb.' So a little while later, in her room, she gathered Valery on her lap and warmly said, 'I'm so sorry about your auntie, love. I expect you'll miss her a lot.' 'Oh no!' said Valery, putting her right. 'We've got *lots* of them!'

So I told both these stories in Liverpool. And somebody said that the grandmother of one of the children in her class had been agonizingly ill for a long time. And when the mother did not expect her to last out the weekend, she asked the teacher please would she take Marian home with her? The teacher did so, and on the Saturday morning the mother phoned her; the grandmother had died. The mother was very upset; she couldn't bear to tell the child herself; there was a deep bond between the child and the grandmother. Please would the teacher break it to her?

All day the teacher tried to think how to tell Marian. By evening, she still didn't know. She decided to give the child a specially nice supper, read her a pleasant story, make sure she had a good rest, and tell her in the morning. All night the teacher lay awake. In the morning after breakfast, utterly exhausted, she told her. 'Then can *I* sleep in the big bed!' cried Marian eagerly.

Funnily enough, someone gave me a copy of Chukovsky's *Two to Five*, and there, in that stilted translation, among the things *Russian* children had said in his hearing I found:

Granny, will you die?

Yes, I will die.

And will you be buried?

Yes, I will be buried.

Deep?

Yes, deep.

Then, Granny, can *I* have the sewing machine?

So in York I told *all* these stories. And a teacher told me about a small boy who said to her, 'Miss, my Nan's dead. We had the funeral Saturday. . . . And we had a *smashing* knees-up after!'

13

I talked some time ago to someone who teaches groups of
backward readers in a junior school. She is well qualified, but not
in a way the teachers' union accepts. She managed to get taken on
as 'medical personnel'; this enabled inadequate teachers in
advance to deal disparagingly with any success she was likely to
have. ('Oh, of course it's all right for *her*. She doesn't have to . . .'
etc. etc.)

She found that the teachers maintained that reading had
nothing to do with them ('the children should *know* how to read')
and could not bear a child to touch them ('it makes me feel sick').

One day, one of her boys went home for his dinner-money just
in time to see his father brought out on a stretcher – he had put
his head in the gas oven. The boy, feeling warmly towards her,
told her about it in distress, when he came back. The teachers
were extremely hostile. 'He has no right to tell you such things.
And you have no right to encourage him.'

Once, when working with a group of children from problem
families, the same group who preferred pretend tea to real tea, I
tried to explain to a social worker of a supposedly non-
authoritarian organization why I was writing the children's names
on chairs, on hooks, on the wall, on table mats, on everything
possible, in every colour of the rainbow; they were the only
under-fives I have ever met who made no response to the sound
of their own name: 'I'm trying to get them to know their own
identity,' I said. 'Oh, but is that a good idea,' she said, 'when each
family only has one or two rooms to live in? If the children have
their own identity, it's going to cause a lot of trouble.' Of course
her logic was right, though her aims in life seemed to be
different from mine . . . an example, if I needed one, of how
extremes meet, or, to be more explicit, of how authoritarians and
non-authoritarians can join hands to confirm the *status quo*,
jointly turning the key.

To such people, love is as disturbing as violence (because both cock a snook at outside authority). People who serve the state in a mediator capacity – teachers, social workers and so on – frequently try to link young people into *safe* relationships (i.e. relationships that will support the *status quo*), fearing that otherwise they will make natural ones which are 'unsafe'. They are terribly afraid of what they call 'unattached youth'; but that this is not concern for a young person's loneliness is shown by the fervent distaste with which they try to separate young people from attachments of their own choice, which social workers sometimes refer to, in words no doubt intended to sterilize fizzing bacilli, as 'pairing'.

You see the results of this clamping down on children's emotional experience, including love, all around us. I was in a Classic cinema some years ago, in a working-class area, which was showing *The L-Shaped Room*. I was not at the time, I remember, struck by any element of stark shocking realism in the film; the abortion scene I thought naïvely unreal. But the main quality in it was then revolutionary – it was the tenderness of teenagers, which extended into tender physical lovemaking.

In the middle of such a love scene (still then unusual in English-speaking cinema), a boy in front, teenage, suddenly farted, very loudly and forcefully. A roar of laughter went up from his mates. Another one farted. Then they all joined in, about ten youths, all straining hysterically to fart as loudly as possible.

The fear in the cinema was almost palpable; but of course no one spoke. The tension was so great you might have thought the boys were firing off revolvers. The audience was paralysed. At such times any action takes on a heroic quality; so a middle-aged usherette heroically got the manager. And the manager ordered them to leave. They argued back. Eventually, with a deafening amount of noise, they got up, each one slamming his seat, slamming each seat in the row as he passed along, and slamming each seat in the long aisle as he moved towards the exit.

When all had gone the general relief was as palpable as the fear, and again unvoiced. And at the end of the performance the entire audience stood at rigid attention for the national anthem. This was something I have never seen in that cinema before or since.

Striving futilely to get out of this suddenly constipatedly patriotic cinema, I wondered how such adults can help young people. The boys' nerves were on edge; they had never been encouraged to be at one with their feelings; their feelings frighten them; and they wonder whether they dare risk growing up if it involves experiences such as this which they do not feel competent for. Will their feelings frighten them less because they have managed to distract attention from them by their destructiveness; and is banging about and farting the best way of getting rid of fear; and will adults whose only reaction to disturbance is a ludicrous authoritarian unity dare to understand them?

This repression of tenderness is still extraordinarily strong in England (the original young hippy generation, making love not war,* were our most vital revolutionary force, before the commercial boys began to make a packet out of their beautiful friendship with them). You see men slowly turning a knob or moving a lever, their head cocked on one side in intense concentration, feeling, listening, delicately and tenderly synchronizing their movement, their behaviour, with the response they get. You rarely see them behaving like this with a fellow human being. Who'd waste such delicate togetherness on a *person*?

A town-hall official almost choked with outrage when two librarian friends of ours – married, as it happened – turned up for a job, and waited in the corridor hand in hand. 'We don't allow *cuddling* here!' he stuttered through clenched teeth. Unfortunately for Michael when he got into the interview room, the official was the interviewer. So since Michael was the only one with qualifications, and since Michael was evidently beyond the pale, the vacancy was left unfilled. Can't let emotional people mix with our books. Bad enough that emotional people write them.

* Actually a Young Liberal Slogan.

14

I was sitting in a railway carriage. A young mother and father came in, with a baby about a year old. The mother settled the baby by the window.

Outside the window stood the mother's parents. Through the glass they chattered, cooed, laughed at the baby, ran their fingers up the window, and called. They were concerned only, and completely, with the baby. The young mother was very silent.

When the train began to pull out of the station, and the grandparents waved to the baby, waving until they were out of sight, the mother spoke to the baby with satisfaction. 'Nan gone. Nan gone,' and instructed the baby to repeat it several times.

Tucked into the corner, on a long journey, as dark came on I watched in the mirror of my window.

Now the baby sat in her young mother's lap. But the baby wanted to stand. There was space on the seat next to her, and the baby reached out for it with one woolly leg. The young mother with a deep suffering sigh that established her status as an adult and her unimpeachable moral position as a mother sat the baby on the seat.

But the baby didn't want to sit. She wanted to stretch her legs, to feel her developing power. She tried to stand. The mother slapped her – not hard, just enough to condition her not to react to impulses – and took her again on her lap. The baby cried.

The father took a cigarette packet from his pocket and gave it to the baby. The baby was interested, shook it, explored it with her mouth, then – still exploringly – gave it to her father. He held it, then handed it back. She shouted for joy, and gave it to him again. This went on a few times, backwards and forwards, now becoming very absorbed. Then, changing her pattern experimentally, she offered it to a surprised young man opposite, who took it, thanked her and handed it back. Again, delight, followed by absorption. Soon half the carriage was involved, like a folk-dance chain. The baby gave to one, and that one gave to another, and that one gave to another, until finally it returned to the baby, who gave again, with a grave joy. It was magical . . . the rhythm of life.

Then the mother took the packet away from her and gave it back to the father, saying sharply though quietly, 'Put it away.' He did so. The baby cried. The mother slapped her. The father read his newspaper. Everyone retreated and read their newspaper.

I suppose the mother would have said, rationalizing, that the baby was being a nuisance. But she wasn't. Everyone was flattered at being included by the baby. Well, she would *become* a nuisance, the mother would have said, righteously, and implying concern for society as a whole.

But the mother was unconsciously playing out the scene with her parents at the station, her anger and jealousy at the bond between them and the baby. Yet what emerged from this immaturity was a demonstration of training in obedience which our society approves. It was sad for the other passengers, as well as for the baby, since they had – through the baby – begun to live spontaneously, creatively and cooperatively, but doubtless most of them received it with resignation, as the way life is and must be.

We all have this tendency to make other people play parts in our own drama; sometimes they haven't seen the script, and sometimes don't even know what the play is. This is hard on husbands, wives, children, pupils. I have done it myself. Once a mother brought her two and a half year old boy to my nursery school. Unfortunately she said she very much wanted him to come because she knew how much I could accomplish. At that time I was pursuing another fantasy in which it was vital for me to be omnipotent, but in which I was failing (I was nursing someone dying of cancer); so I rose instantly to the new challenge, a second string. The poor child was not ready to come to a nursery school, at least not to stay in one without his mother. He screamed frantically whenever she left the room. In any other circumstances I would have said so. But this mother had, at a particular moment, saying a particular line, hurled her child into my personal drama; and the child suffered for it. I met him a couple of times later on, and I must say he didn't seem to bear me any grudge. Small children are sometimes more forgiving than one deserves, and more resilient . . . for a while at any rate.

(The day after this train journey, a letter arrived from Bob, in a little village in South India. By chance he wrote: 'I've just exchanged bits of twig with a small girl who's been hanging around. She wouldn't accept mine at first, but she imitated me offering it and I accepted it from her and put it away. Then I offered her a bit again and she took it. Now she's gone home. Sometimes they touch me not quite accidentally, mutter surreptitiously English phrases – Kumhea, goot moning, one two tree. Smiling behind their eyebrows.' Again that natural rhythm of growth, reaching out, disappearing, reappearing . . . and always a little further on. Like Nina's eleven, twelve and thirteen year olds in the one o'clock club, who were using a babyhood pattern they had probably never been allowed to savour in order to bring themselves more up to date in their lives.)

How does this natural rhythm of children ever survive the shock of our Western-style birth, with its tension and convulsion and its slap on the bare buttocks, and the noise and constant lights of the maternity hospital, and its authoritarian child-rearing? Outside in our garden is a baby in a pram, just as he always is – hood up whatever the weather, strapped in, dummy in mouth – chained, gagged and in a walled cell – sight, sound, movement all forbidden. Yet it is amazing what that human baby of a year and a half can manage to do against those odds. In a few minutes everything is out of the pram, he is making gurgling noises behind his dummy, and straining on his knees to get hold of the top of the hood and peer over it. The determination, the energy, the urge to assert human-ness seem indomitable. Presently his mother will come out and he won't half get a whack. She is determined he shall look nice and behave properly.

I once sat in an expensive Cornish hotel where the outlook was picturesque and the food famous. At the next table were a mother and father, two children aged about eleven and thirteen, and a baby in a high chair. The mother was feeding the baby. When she gave him a piece of bread and butter, she held it up in the air, away from his clutching hand, until the baby said 'Please' – or rather, a sound that she agreed to accept as an attempt at 'Please', for the baby was too young to talk. When she put the bread in his hand he had to say 'Thank you', or something like it, or she took it away again. The whole family joined in – 'Say please! Please! Please!' the children insisted in chorus, like squawking rooks on a tree (they had been through this once, and they were glad now to be on the winning side), and the father looked suddenly out from behind his paper and added his own stern order to mark his status; and the baby looked at them in a frightened anxious way and back at the piece of bread that was denied him, and tried to do, hit or miss, this magic imperative meaningless thing. In the middle of all this nervous strain he burped, and the shrieks of horror that went up startled me, never mind the baby. He jumped in his high chair, shivered, looked round as if for an escape, then apprehensively put his fat pudgy hand over his mouth. 'Excuse me! Excuse me!' they all shouted righteously. And after that they forgave him, and allowed him to have another bite of bread and butter.

There are different ways of doing this. Some 'progressive' middle-class people go in for conning; they even con themselves. A three year old and her mother had been asked out to tea. 'May I get down, Mummy?' asked the bored child. 'Of course, darling,' said the mother, with emphatic sweetness. Why 'of course', since the child knew she had to ask?

Some groups are less saccharine. I knew two parents who worked on the buses; the mother was ruthlessly determined, for reasons of her own – her private drama was a very fascinating, spell-binding one – to groom the child for 'better' society. She had plans. And because of these plans she would never allow this eighteen month old to cry – whether for physical hurt or for spiritual hurt. When she left her husband – who adored the child and whom the child adored – and took the child with her, she told the child in her implacable voice that had warnings in it, 'You don't love your Daddy any more. Do you?' And shivering in all his body, the child shook his head.

When this natural rhythm is distorted by the interference of adults who are following a private script, anger sets in.

Eight years ago a child was playing in our garden with a dozen others. He had a wonderful sweet serenity. At two, he played happily and absorbedly by himself, singing all the while his own meandering off-key songs, looking up as I passed with a beaming, slightly absent-minded smile, and occasionally getting to his feet and coming to tell me something quick and confidential and gleeful, and returning to his work again. And now at three he was no longer a child happily alone among other noisy children, but a child aware of others.

His parents were two charming, elegant and cultured people, a pleasure to look at. I said to his mother once, 'I wonder if you know how lucky you are having such a tranquil child.' The look she gave me startled me. It seemed at home Julian fought, bit, kicked, scratched, like a child possessed.

That afternoon his father came into the garden to take him home, and I saw at once why. I saw Julian's face and body change before my eyes like the transformation scene in Jekyll and Hyde. The child had got to his feet happily when his father came, had stepped out of the sandpit and come singing and dancing gravely over the grass, with not a word to anybody but with a grace in his whole light singing body that said to the world, 'We are happy together. We love each other. Everything is at peace.' He was halfway across the grass to the gate, when I called to him, 'Julian – you've forgotten your little car.' Unspeaking still he gravely wheeled in his dancing, describing an absorbed arc, and danced back to me still singing. He took his car from my hand as he skirted me, as a Cossack on horseback picks up a handkerchief, but dreamily and meditatively. I smiled at him as he danced away again.

Then his father said, 'Julian!' Still he danced and sang. 'Julian!' Still he went on . . . but not so certainly now, for the world was breaking in. 'Julian! Say "Thank you".' The singing faltered. 'Say "Thank you".' The dancer stumbled. The dancer's legs were suddenly heavy. 'Julian!'

Faltering, all grace and strength and beauty gone, the child turned round. His father took hold of his arm – not violently, for

he was a cultured man, but with a grip that was not to be thrown off – and brought him to me. I saw the child's face and body change from a relaxed, loving and thanksgiving tranquillity, to taut, sullen contorted hate. It was *my* relationship, the casual, unsought understanding between the child and myself, that was being utterly destroyed. I could not bear to see it, nor be associated with it. I rumpled the child's hair, pushed him lightly away, and walked quickly away to the other end of the garden where the other children were playing.

I do not know if he ever said the socially acceptable words 'Thank you'. I do know that his face and body had had more spontaneous 'Thank you' in them than any words could ever express. He would have been happy one day to put this into words, which he would have picked up from pleasant adults around him, and would have taken a pleasure in the verbal translation as one does in any creative skill. But his successful, cultured and conformist father dared not trust.

A great deal was expected of Julian. I had already been told he had been entered for the same preparatory and public schools that his father had gone to. The father's parents lived near them in an architect-designed house, perhaps too near. Success, in terms of money, power and a beautiful cultured surface, was what was in the family's mind when they looked at Julian – *not Julian*. They never saw the vital loving child in front of them. Small wonder he hated them, and smashed their expensive glassware and pottery.

15

Mrs Hill was nineteen when she took a flat in our house, and John was five months old. She was a pretty tiny child-wife, who had never had childhood, and she treated John like a prettily dressed-up doll. Maybe she had never had a doll; or maybe she had never had the time or the solitude or the permission to beat it. So she played out her lost childhood with a real live baby whom she never wanted or realized completely she would have.

In their flat upstairs alone with the baby she would talk all the time. She was pretending to talk to the baby, but she was talking at the top of her voice, making you aware of her existence. She always left all the doors open, and tried to conduct her whole life on the landing, banging and clattering and knocking everything over in case you had forgotten her for a moment. I think she hits John so much and makes him scream, so that you know she is there, and therefore she knows she is alive. A scream from John means to the house at large – 'I, Daphne Hill, am here! Remember me!' (How many people – healthy children and immature adults – are insisting with this destructive anger, 'See me!')

Her own mother, she told me, abandoned the family and went off with another man. Mrs Hill talks about her as if she was a prostitute; maybe she was. Her father . . . well, she says she gave evidence in court against him, but I am not really sure whether it was for incest or pretended incest or longed-for incest. I shouldn't think she has had any love; and this always brings about a sort of manipulating attempt to get some kind of approximation of it, almost out of curiosity. She says she brought up her kid sister herself, and now her mother has written to her and told her she must get her young sister away from her father because she's getting a big girl and he'll start on her next. But you can see she hankers after her father, almost admires him, the father she says she gave evidence against. It is impossible to tell when she is fantasizing; occasionally I have assumed, quite amiably and privately, that what she was saying was fantasy, and later have found uncontrovertibly that it was true; fantasy and reality are interwoven, impossible to distinguish without research. She says she hits John all the time because her father always hit her.

At first she would tell me tearfully how John had a weak heart – the doctor in hospital had said so. It is hard to say whether this is true; I think it is part of her constant fight against anonymity, and also a wish, a secret hope, of hers. If it is really true, she is trying to kill him. I think myself it is not true; she only wishes it; her pretty tears at the sadness of it are an expression of hate.

He would always be falling off the bed, and the crash and the screaming would resound through the house. I'd say, 'Why don't you put chairs round it so that he can't fall off? Or why don't you put him on the floor?' She would just laugh a little, and I could understand why she laughed for we were talking from two different standpoints. He used to fall downstairs too, all the way to the bottom sometimes. The first time she was very hysterical, screaming even louder than the baby, and my husband and I took them both to hospital. I think she enjoyed the outing, that and the feeling of being looked after (not *being* looked after, but the *feeling* of being looked after; it is the sensation of it that interests her). The second time he fell, only halfway this time, I heard her say later with a laugh, 'He's frightened of the stairs now. Good job!'

She used to slam John savagely into his high chair and shove a spoonful of food into his mouth. He would turn it round on his tongue, wondering at its unfamiliarity, and push a little of it out as babies do. She would slap him. He would cry, and all the rest of the food in his mouth would dribble out with his tears. She would scream at him and slap him again, shovelling food into his mouth, shouting, 'Eat it up, you little pig!' Then he would vomit everything up hysterically. She would slap him over and over again, seize him, rush him into the other room, slam him into the cot, pull up the sides with a furious clatter, shouting 'You stay there! You'll get *nothing* now!' and crash the door to, leaving him sobbing and gasping for breath. Then as likely as not she would come sobbing down to me – 'I don't know what I do wrong! I'm

sure I've done my best for him !' And I would advise and
suggest and help, out of compassion for each of them. But I know
she does not want help, advice or suggestion, or anything that will
presuppose action by her and would end with her standing on her
own feet. She just trails her failures in front of me, almost
coquettishly, and she does not want me to take them away. What
she wants from me is a substitute love ; and I am aware all the
time, all the time she is wearing me out, that I can never give her
the real thing or ever give her enough of the substitute, that I can
never close up the empty gap of her childhood ; and because of
this, in her tearful acceptance of everything I do for her there is
always the possible flash of the flick-knife, always the flicker of
betrayal. Whatever vile thing she may say about me elsewhere will
never surprise me.

Now she has two babies. She didn't want the second one. 'He
doesn't get his other women pregnant, but he gets me pregnant
all right,' she said, and in her anger there was a certain satisfaction
at being picked out for this abuse. The weeks after he was born,
when she stayed at home to look after the two of them, were
among the most appalling in my life. Day after day the walls of the
house would be quivering with hysteria ; the air would be leaping
with screams and the sound of blows. It was impossible for me to
work. I moved all round the house to get away from it. For weeks
I worked in the cellar. Sometimes I would give up all thought of
working, and go up to her. 'You lie down and have a rest – or go
out for a walk and look at the shops. I'll look after John for a
while.' I would bring him down. He would shake and gasp with
sobs, and I would put him on the kitchen floor and give him
interesting things to play with. He would want to play with
them ; I could see they were drawing him ; but how could he play,
when he could hear his mother moving about upstairs – the
mother who filled him with terror and desolation but was so
necessary to him ? I thought I had rescued him but I had only
connived at his exile. I thought I was the friend, but I was the
judge and the jailer. He would half-crawl, half-totter to the door,
sobbing, give a backward fleeting glance at the playthings he

would have liked to give himself to but dare not, and howl, howl, for his howling mother.

He would not have been upstairs again long when I would hear a clatter, a resounding slap, a scream, a shout, several more loud slaps followed by screams from John and screams from her, and I would come out into the hall to find John sobbing, and Mrs Hill, weeping on second thoughts too, on the landing. And I would suggest things.

But I am not making the right response. All this thinking, when a few good smacks, plenty of them, would be a lot quicker. (But would they? She slaps, slaps, and I hear her shouting at him, 'Don't you *dare*! Don't you dare defy me!' because in spite of the continuous blows this baby still has the spirit to defy her and will only stop defying her when his spirit is broken and he is less than a whole human being and partly destroyed). This way of thinking things out, considering alternatives, then choosing the one that seems best, is quite alien to her. Her parents never introduced her to it, nor did her teachers – indeed they couldn't have done, since choice in tranquillity presupposes a basis of love. Why should she be expected to start now, in somebody else's house, with two kids already though she's not yet twenty-one, and all the hire-purchase instalments and people coming to take things away and banging on the door all the time for money so she has to pretend she isn't in? Hasn't she got enough on her plate without thinking?

And besides, like some teachers in slum districts who have helped to condition her, she believes the world is a hard place for kids like her's and the sooner they feel its hardness the better; she felt it; let him feel it too, the little devil; she will provide it. In any case, I am simply giving her advice again, and advice is irrelevant to her emptiness when what she is doing is trailing actions for an exciting response.

When John was trying to stand, reaching up to the coffee table or a chair to pull himself up, she would slap him so that he fell. ('Leaving finger-marks!') When he reached out in wonder to a flower in a vase, she would slap him. I thought she was afraid of him pulling off the petals, till I realized her flowers were plastic. She will not let him do anything, will not let him grow. She would

hit him when he wet his nappy, so he would pull his nappy off
to wet, and she would hit him harder ; he doesn't know what she
wants of him.

Most of the time he is screaming. Soon he began very accurately
to reproduce her roar, but without words. She roared at him, he
roared back at her. In time, she began to notice it too, and was
amused, almost flattered. So then, when she wasn't angrily
roaring at him and having him roar back, she would be pretending
to roar at him in order to make him roar back. When she was
pretending, she laughed when he roared back. When she wasn't
pretending, she hit him, and he . . . and then she . . . roared some
more. Sometimes in the middle of a laugh at him, she would
change to a roar, and then a slap would crack through the house.
Nothing was predictable. There must be so many children brought
up like this. The only way they know what they are doing is
approved of, is if the slap does not come ; but of course it may
only be delayed ; they never can tell.

The noise, the chaotic hysterical unhappiness of it, was
unbelievable. She decided to bring an end to this situation by
putting her head in the gas oven. She timed it competently.
Perhaps she set everything ready and then leaned out of the
window first to make sure her husband was coming. I had
suspected something was brewing because for a little while
the house had been quiet ; and this was so disturbing and strange
that now it was the quiet that stopped me from working.

It was not at all a cry for help, a signal sent up from a ship
sinking in a boiling sea. Help, as I have said, is not what she
wants. It was a demand for an attention that does not involve any
real relationship, any reciprocity, any growth. It was a threat, and
it worked, because her husband agreed she should get a job again
and park the two babies somewhere during the day. I was relieved
when it worked. In fact, while the doctor was phoning for an
ambulance at my desk I urged this on Mr Hill. ('She's still a child !'
I said. 'She should never have had two babies !') I was afraid she
might take John in the gas oven with her the second time, since
her husband was fond of him while not so fond of her. And

anyway I thought she might stop screaming and throwing crockery at her husband if she'd been out all day ; I thought she would be happier, and that might help everyone.

So now John is with his third minder. He is not yet two, but apart from having had three minders, he has already been with Council foster parents twice, when Mrs Hill abandoned the family completely before she hit on the better tactic of the gas oven.

Now when he comes down here, he no longer tries to get back to her in fear of being abandoned. If he hears her coming after him, he frenziedly starts to slam all the doors between him and her, slamming the last one hysterically in her face. This franticness is his present keynote. He could not concentrate on anything before because of anxiety, but at least that drew him in one direction, back to her. Now he cannot concentrate because of a wild chaos that is in him ; he has no direction, only a frenzied wildness. He snatches at things and throws them down because he is snatching at something else, and he dare not stay to look at any of them because he seems always to have her ghost behind him driving him on. The tranquil absorption that you see in other children of nearly two that enables them to explore the world never shows in him. Sometimes you cannot get through to him. 'John,' you say, 'John.' But he cannot hear you for the clanging bells in his head. I take hold of him – he fights frantically to get away – and I say quietly but insistently, 'John. John. *John*,' and eventually he hears me. But still he does not understand me.

The other day when she was hitting John on the stairs I came out to her and said, 'Till you came here, no one in this house ever hit babies. You scarcely see the two of them now except at weekends, and you can't even be kind to them then. I've done all I can to help, but if I can't stop you hitting John then you'll have to hit him in a different house.'

So now she has stopped hitting him – I think ; she only screams at him. 'Shurrup ! I'll kill you ! My God, you want a bloody good hiding ! I never want to see you ! I'll give you a bloody good belting ! Stop it ! Eat it ! Eat it, you little pig ! Shurrup !' If he stops yelling, she goes on shouting 'Shurrup ! Shurrup !' until he starts again.

I don't know if this is an advance. Today he came down here with his face covered in bruises, his nose streaming with blood. I asked her why John's nose was bleeding and she said he had fallen off the bed. I am not saying she has beaten him up, but maybe she helped him or provoked him or made it easy for him to fall off the bed, and maybe she felt a certain satisfaction when he did...

If you saw these two out together, clean, tidy, prettily dressed, you wouldn't turn round to look at them, they would be so conformist. I think all over London, maybe all over England, there are babies growing up in their deprivation into children who think they are not loved unless they are shouted at and beaten, and adults who think they are not cherished unless they are betrayed. They will buy things on hire purchase and never pay the instalments, because dimly they feel the world owes them something, that they have a right to something that was never freely given; and all the bangings on the door and all the court summonses are only their own shouting parents whom they learned, when they could, to hide away from at such crises. They will have no natural concern for others and will only behave well when they are threatened by powerful people. Tranquillity will frighten them by its lack of response, and in silence they will only be aware of their heart beating louder and louder. So they will shout for the rest of their life and make clattering, clanging drama out of nothing, even if it destroys them.

Or perhaps instead they will withdraw into a secret psychopathic shell where they feel nothing and hear nothing, and maybe get a subtle cunning revenge from frustrating their tormenters by insanity, the last weapon. But these will be fewer, and they will be noticed.

That was far as my notes went. It is hard to remember the second baby's name now, because she never called him by it. She used to leave him in places. She would go out with him and come back without him, and I'd say, fear secretly catching me,

'What have you done with him?' and she'd laugh and say, 'I've left him at the hospital. He's got a cold. I'll go back for him in two or three weeks.' How she brought it off beats me.

He would sit in his pram in the garden, unmoving. Once I went out and stroked his bare arm with one finger. He looked at me for a long time, and then gradually he fathomed that something vague was breaking through to him from his arm, and he looked down at it, trying to make some correlation between my finger, his skin and the sensation; but his face showed no interest; there was no delight; he had not even broken through into curiosity – just a vague need. . . . But when I stopped stroking and came indoors, he cried. He felt he had been deprived of this thing he had not been able to grasp when he had it; it was very pitiful. He cries very strangely, a high-pitched eerie bodiless wailing that is not like a child at all . . . spine-chilling. I think John will end up in Borstal, this one in a psychiatric ward.*

She left her husband three times during this period, sometimes with the children, sometimes without. In between, she left them with numerous minders; this enabled her to be shocked at the minders' 'not looking after them properly' so that she could feel good and loving. She became pregnant a third time, went to a hospital to ask for a National Health abortion, and when she was about four and a half months pregnant and they were still conning her ('observing' her, they called it) she went berserk and smashed the place up; so they gave her an abortion, then. She came home haggard, a child with black holes for eyes. Soon after this we found her another flat, bigger, with a garden. We couldn't stand it any longer. What was appalling me most was that my fingers were beginning to itch too. I too was secretly beginning to want to hit John and scream at him. For though he was only two, not yet in school, not yet in the psychopathic ward, not yet in Borstal, hitting and screaming had already made him into a child whom soon everyone would hit and scream at. That is really what his mother wanted, and she would get her way, because, make no mistake, society would be behind her, and that too was what his mother wanted and needed, to have society approving her, sympathizing with her, paying attention.

(In Islington, I knew a boy called Tommy. Tommy's father used to beat them all up, Tommy and his nine brothers and sisters and

* Later I learned that the difference (withdrawn, frenetic) was due only to age.

his suicidal mother; when he was exhausted from belting them all, he lived alone and morosely in his own room. Tommy is now in Borstal. He hit a teacher who had hit his young brother. The magistrate said to Tommy – and I wrote it down – 'It is a pity that someone can't take a birch-rod and give you a thorough good hiding. That is the thing you need more than anything else, and if it had been done early enough you wouldn't be here today. . . . How people keep their hands off people like you, I just don't know.')

But John's mother didn't like the new flat. She was lonely and isolated; she kept phoning me and crying.

One day, when she was about twenty-three, I heard she was dead. She had got pregnant again, gone to a hospital again for an abortion; they played the same game as before, and kept her in 'to save the baby'; at Christmas, overwhelmed with sentimentality, or cynically pretending so in order to get peace and quiet, they let her go home for the holiday; whereupon she did – or got done – what she considered necessary and was brought back to hospital in an ambulance, 'kept on ice for five days' her friend told me, and died. Her husband played cards and drank beer merrily at the funeral gathering. The debt-collectors still come to our house looking for him. They go to the flat too but they can never find him; nor can the policeman whose young daughter he has got pregnant. Nor can we, to whom he owes a hundred pounds or so.

The last debt-collector to come to our house asked about 'the deceased Mr Hill'. It seems he now goes as dead too. I was sceptical and sardonic. So, on my encouragement, was the debt-collector. He told me black comedy stories about men who were dead when he called round, and sitting at the kitchen table having a beer when he nipped back ten minutes later. But he didn't have time to catch them all out. So officially John's father is dead, all debts wiped out, home hath gone and ta'en his wages, free now to start up little third-rate rackets elsewhere.

But she, touching, appalling, destructive and destroyed child-mother, is truly dead.

And the children live on, both officially alive, in institutions, I suppose. Maybe not even in the same one.

16

Steve is another London parent. I first talked to him in the semi-darkness of his flat, in a black East-End street.

His own father I knew had treated him savagely when he was a child, but this was something he didn't tell me much about. 'I'm generally a better talker than this,' he said apologetically, 'but I don't talk about that time of my life very much, because I don't like talking about it. I get a lump in my throat.'

But he told me about the education he got, at the Institution that he and his kid brother were sent to when they were eleven and a half and ten.

'Mind you', he said, 'I don't want to give you the idea I was an angel before I went to that place. My kid brother and I climbed a wall and got into a cake factory and ate a couple of Swiss rolls. That's why we got into court. We were very young, but I do believe if my father had said he would look after us and wanted us, they wouldn't have sent us away. They talked in that court as if they were sending us away to somewhere wonderful. "You'll be well looked after," they said. "People will be kind to you. You'll get a good education."'

I was sitting on a couch while he talked to me, and Davy, a baby of fourteen months, was beside me. The baby had taken from the shelves opposite about twenty books, one by one, some of them very large, and brought them over to lie in a pile at the foot of the couch, and, lying on his stomach – he was naked except for a very short cardigan – his body and legs thrashing wildly in the air to keep his balance, grunting and panting with effort he strained over the side of the couch, and one by one picked up each book – some of them so heavy that they crashed down again, once, twice, three times, before he managed to lug each up by a corner all the way. Then he sat up each time and wriggled round, and pushed them one by one behind the hard cushion of the couch.

It was an enormous task he had set himself, this baby. He did not have to do it. But he carried it right through to a satisfying end.

His legs waved in the air so wildly as he strained down towards the floor, that I worried a little that he might pitch on his head, so very gently I took hold of one foot. I did not want to do it if it wasn't necessary. It was perhaps a hindrance, maybe even an insult, to such a competent human being. So I held it very loosely, ready to tighten if need be; probably it wasn't necessary at all. And when the task was satisfactorily finished, he was instantly eager and fresh for the next.

I watched him, and could not think of any other baby I knew who would be allowed to set himself such a task and carry it through. The baby upstairs would be slapped resoundingly if he showed by a glance he had even thought of making a beginning. So most babies, when they are grown and go to secondary school, will have written on their reports, 'Cannot concentrate.' 'No determination.' 'Will not persevere.' 'Not interested in what he is doing.' That unflagging energy, that tremendous unswerving concentration, that purpose descried and fulfilled – why, an adult could change the whole world with these! But most of us have had it knocked out of us in babyhood. And perhaps indeed authority knows what it is doing for authority's good.

The father enjoyed talking about his baby; he was on the dole and spent a lot of time with him. In the half-darkness he handed his thoughts to me casually, with pleasure, and with complete individuality, as a child will pluck you flowers.

'He's not frightened of the dark,' he said. 'He'll walk through the dark to a voice he knows, as if it was the light. He's never been left in the dark to cry. A small fear . . . sometimes you can't shake it off all your life.

'If you were to take something from him, he'd cry. But if you put out your hand, he'll give it and that's fine.

'We took him to the paddling pool in the little park down the road, a month ago. He had nothing on. I saw the keeper talking to some people, and then he came over to us and said, "Get some trunks on that child!" I said, "What did you say?" He talked a bit more politely then. "Well . . . I asked you to get some trunks on him." I said, "Why?" He said, "Well . . . you know how it is . . . people get embarrassed, you know . . ." I said, "Well, let them be embarrassed if that's how they are." "Well look, chum –" "If you can show me anything in the park regulations that says he must wear trunks . . ." "Well no, there isn't anything." In the end he went away. The people around looked daggers at me – women from round here!' (He laughed and shook his head. He wasn't angry with them.)

'He likes to drag clothes about, throwing them around. He likes jumping up and down on newspaper, fitting tins inside each other, playing with gramophone records and pencils. No bought toy is any use to him.

'People are funny about a baby playing with things that aren't toys and breaking them. It's not that the people are cruel, or even unkind. And if you said to them, "Look, that cup you're making such a fuss about only cost sixpence, against a growing child," they'd know it was silly. But it isn't that. It's their possession, that's what worries them.

'A cot is like a prison to him. Even when he's sleeping and he half wakes and sees the bars, he cries. We take him out. Even in his little chair that we put him in to have something from a bowl, after a couple of minutes he wants to be out, and he walks about holding a piece of bread or something in his hand. I think too he needs to feel he's sharing with us, and doing what we do. If we give him his dinner in a bowl when we're having ours on plates, he doesn't want it. If we put his food on our plates and let him have it from there, then he's happy.

'The world must look quite different to a baby. People don't think about this. They just see it their way.

'He has a mouth organ and a little Indian bamboo flute. He loves them both. He loves music. If I put on a record, he recognizes those two instruments, and stops whatever he's doing and looks, and listens very intently.

'He doesn't like to be picked up much and held. He will climb up on your lap himself and get down himself when he wants to. We went to someone's house recently, and there were expensive things there. We had to hold him and he didn't like it. We didn't stay long.

'It's easy to underestimate a child's intelligence. As soon as a child gets old enough to understand what grown-ups are saying, he gets sent out of the room. I don't think I'd ever say anything I didn't want Davy to hear. Of course, a child might be confused because he didn't fully understand what he'd heard, and you'd need to explain it more to get rid of his anxiety. But I think the child would ask, if he was confused, if he knew you would always tell him.

'We develop a strength to withstand certain bumps – because there are bound to be bumps – if things are not forced on us.

'Children talk to me about things their mothers and fathers have no idea they know anything about.

'As a child, you value yourself as other people value you. If your parents call you a brat all the time, you really believe you must be a brat, and you can't figure out why you in particular should be such a brat.

When we play with him, we play quite rough. We throw him up in the air. We run very fast. He shrieks with laughter. Of course sometimes he hurts us, scratches our face, perhaps. There's nothing you can do about it.

'If we want him to go to sleep, we all pretend to go to sleep.

'When he has a bath, he screams when he has to come out. But he's grown out of that.

'He wants to do everything for himself. Even things he can't do, like putting on his shoes or buttoning his coat, he wants to do himself. We have to do it very quickly. He'll quite often do what you want him to, if you let him do it on his own.

'He's left by himself for a few minutes at a time, that's all. A few months ago, you couldn't walk out of the door. Whereas months before that, he would play happily on the floor, not even noticing you'd gone into the other room. Now he notices you've gone, but he knows you will come back.

'I would never send him to a one-sex school – I'd sooner go to prison.'

I had never met before, in a young man of his age, such a tender, confident, understanding attitude to growth. Where did it come from? His father didn't develop it, with his belt and buckle. Was it his school then, the 'good education' and the 'kind' people that the magistrate told him about? He talked of them.

'When I first went there, I couldn't get the education I wanted – it was much lower education than I'd had in the day-school. I wanted to be taught.

'We used to get up at about 7 or 7.30. Someone strode through the dormitory shouting, "Everybody out of bed." You had to jump out – if you didn't your whole bed would be on the floor – and rush about like a lunatic. Everything was timed like in the army. You had to stand to attention when you were ready. The last two or three – I couldn't understand this, someone had to be last – were put on a special work party.

'From there you marched into the assembly hall. You had a number, and when you'd washed you lined up before what we called the screw. If any speck of dirt was found behind your ear or your nail, you got swiped and sent back.

'When everyone was washed and ready we were sent to have a meal. Some of the masters allowed you to talk quietly. Some not at all. But those that let you talk quietly stopped you talking at once if your voices got too loud.

'We were seven at a table. Some of us served the food to the rest. You were allowed, I think, ten minutes. Then you had to stand up. If you hadn't eaten your food in that time, you were in for it.

'Then we were marched back to assembly. Then we were split up into different work parties, polishing the dormitories, scrubbing lavatories and so on. Our dormitory ran the whole length of the building. In order to polish it, you had three little rags, one for each knee and one for your two hands. You all got down in a row, with your three rags, with a master shouting, "Left! Right! Left! Right!" you all swinging your hands at the same time on the polish rag from right to left, and shifting your knees back the right fraction, all in army order. If you ever tried to suggest there was a better way of polishing a floor, it was cheek and you were put on report.

'They had a marks system. You had to stay on each grade a certain time before you could move up to the next. The highest grade I ever reached was fifty, for one week. Apart from that I spent most of the time in detention, which was no marks at all.

'It had nothing to do with education. You can see it didn't, because they found six pupils in the whole school who needed more education than they were getting and they formed what they called a grammar group; and I was one.

'You had to be on a certain grade to get privileges like going out for a walk marching in threes, or going home for Christmas. I was never once allowed to go home. I wasn't good enough.

'The main thing the children were punished for was talking. If a master heard anyone talking and didn't know who, he'd pick on anybody just to show you couldn't get away with it.

'All the masters had idiosyncrasies about the way they beat the kids. One used to make you stand to attention and grab you by the nose and pull it till your eyes were streaming, then suddenly let you fall back and punch you in the face, then pull you by the nose again, and all over and over again till you dropped to the floor, with your nose running with blood. One used to beat you over the head with his knuckles. Others used belts, canes.

'Everyone had to be a good footballer, not just play football but be a good footballer. That didn't make sense to me. How can everyone be a good footballer? If you weren't good enough they had you face the wall all afternoon with someone watching you.

'We had constant parades, sometimes for three or four hours. People used to faint, they'd be carried to the washroom, doused and stood to attention extra hours for punishment.

'I was made to join the boxing class. I don't like hurting anyone. I used to punch the punchball but that wasn't good enough. So I matched up with a friend of mine who didn't like the boxing lark either. But it was too obvious that we didn't want to hurt each other, so they took my friend out and put the boxing champion in with me. I tried to tell him not to go for my nose, because I knew I wouldn't be able to stand that – I'd get angry. But he rushed at me, and bang, bang, bang, my nose was pouring with blood. I tore my gloves off and rushed at him – I was really mad. I got six of the best for that in front of the whole school.

'I was very good at art. I made posters, and full-scale models. But I couldn't explain anything. Nobody was interested to know why I was such a bad character and had no grades. I kept asking to stay in to draw and read, but they wouldn't let me. We had to go out and rush about outside. When I went out I would just sit on the stone steps. Still they wouldn't let me stay in.

'At one football game I broke my leg. They wouldn't believe me at first. They stood me up on it. I was screaming.

'The only time I got on all right was when, because of my young brother and his master there, I was put in charge of the annexe where the kids were. But then I broke my leg, and was back.

'All the masters except one made me stand on parade with my leg iron. I had to hop and skip. The plaster was always breaking.

'You couldn't explain anything to anyone. If a master wouldn't listen to you and you went to the head, the head would be furious and you'd get the cane. Several boys ran away. Some ran to the police, but even with bruises and black eyes they wouldn't listen and they took them straight back.

'You weren't there for any set time. They kept me there till I was fifteen years and four months. And during that time, apart from going out in organized walks in twos and threes, I was never out of the place. I never saw a girl all that time.

'I've spent four months in jail for punching a cop, and I'd sooner have jail than that. They don't want to know your name in jail and you can get out of there without a scuff, but no one could go two days in that place without getting a scuff for talking. Two or three times a week you'd be beaten for talking.

'To the visitor the facilities were fantastic. It could look like a paradise. It's kept beautifully. The boys keep it so. Nobody dare walk on a flowerbed. Once I picked an apple from a tree and ate it, and for this I got six of the best in front of the school with my trousers down.

'We had prayers and hymns at the school, no special denomination.

'The teachers to my mind were none of them qualified. They were all of them frustrated. They were none of them the kind of people who should ever have been put in charge of children. They would lose their temper, go red in the face, and beat and beat and beat, till the boy was lying there on the floor. I'm not very good at remembering people's faces, but to this day I remember every one of them, and if I ever saw one of them I'd have to be pulled off to be sure I didn't kill him. You had to develop a good friendship there, with someone, or you'd deteriorate.

'Because of my father – he used to beat me up, you know – I was the sort of boy who wouldn't be *made* to do anything. If I was asked properly of course I would. But they wouldn't. And so they'd beat and beat.

110

'And because I had no grades, they used to have me scrubbing floors instead of doing painting. Once they had me scrape all the dirt out between the cobblestones with a stick and take it away and sift it till it was fine, and then take it back and put it back between the stones. They couldn't think of anything for me to do. I was the permanent one on detention.

'Even after my leg had been healed off, I didn't go back to the annexe. They wouldn't let me. And my young brother came home each Christmas, but not me. There was no one at all you could go to and confide in, and talk out your troubles.

'When I left there, there was nobody to take me. My father was at sea, and my mother was in the process of getting remarried. I told them I wanted to go to sea too, so they sent me to Southampton. I had to stay there till I was sixteen. I worked in a pram factory, and then at last I went to sea.

'I was always interested in people and places, and everything that was different to me was good. Going to sea was an education in itself. I met many people, some very clever people, and they were all men while I was just a boy, and I'd talk and talk.

'I knew nothing about sex before I went to sea. My father kept me completely ignorant. If he saw me walking down the street with a little girl, before I went to school, he'd thrash me for it. What a little boy and girl of eight or nine can do to each other I don't know, but he'd thrash me. I had a hell of a lot to catch up on, and the world was such a peculiarly fascinating place, and they hadn't trained me to come out into a world like this.

'I have a kind of fad, maybe an obsession, for honesty. I always remember saying over and over again, "It wasn't me, it wasn't me." And I could never understand why if you told the truth they wouldn't believe you, when all the time they kept telling you to tell the truth.

'That few years I was at that school was a lifetime. It was a hundred years. I was conscious all the time that it wasn't my life. It was just a matter of obey. Do this. Do that. You couldn't discuss or argue. I could never understand why no one would listen.

'Since I've left that place, I've tried to understand about authority – who does it, what it's for, who benefits by it. And to my mind it's just a racket. People are born to live down a hole and work down that hole and stay in it till you die. I know it was like that for me, and I know it's like that for thousands of other people.

'My father used to work sixteen hours a day for thirty bob a week in the slump. He was a terrible father, but I bear no malice. He was a victim of the way he was having to live. When I was a kid I used to wish he was dead; and if I had the courage I suppose I would have tried to kill him. But now I don't bear him a grudge. What chance have people like that?

'I wouldn't let go. All those beatings, I took because I was hanging on to my individuality. The others were like sheep.

'They taught us religion. I thought, how can they tell us these things when they are beating us up all the time? So I began to study religion, to see what sense there was in it. I think Jesus was a fantastic man with a terrific philosophy, but I don't believe he was magic. But the church has used religion as a weapon to make people do what they're told, and plunder and murder for what they are told. I've been in Naples and seen people without shoes stealing, and if you catch them at it they fight as if they were fighting for their lives. But the church there has gold in it.

'Two out of every three masters at that school were messing about sexually with the boys. Yet I remember once two of the boys were caught together, and they were thrashed in front of the school. The toilets had doors only that high – two or three feet – and these masters would come round all the time, looking in.

'I've got a shocking temper. It's in my mind all the time. I would hate ever to hurt anyone.

'I've read books on psychology. I wanted to understand myself and other people. I dug into that a lot. Even politics I had to dig into, because it's all part of the same thing, and I had to know. I was sent to this place because of the courts, and the courts are part of the government, so I had to see how this could have happened. It's amazing how the Establishment can use ordinary people against other ordinary people.

'I used to love to see films about schools that had these terrifically understanding masters.'

I put all this down in detail at the time, because I thought it was important. I have not tidied it, shaped it, or prettied it up in any way.

Steve went to prison once or twice. Then he went back to heroin – he had been on it before – and then he voluntarily put his name on a ten-day waiting list and started 'a cure' in a hospital; the cold of heroin withdrawal, colder than any cold that comes at you from outside, shook him from head to foot, and he vomited yellow vomit over and over and over again, and the male nurses always watching him among the long unloving rows of beds reminded him of the warders of his childhood.

He would lift his throbbing head very slowly to talk to me, his fingers pressing into his temples and coming up with his head, as if his fingers lifted his head or his head lifted his fingers, and he said that at the North Pole the cold was outside you and you could lie down in the snow and die and forget it; but not when the cold was inside.

His friends – teenagers, nineteen, twenty years old – used to come to see him. Sometimes they would bring his young wife, a beautiful Trinidadian stripper, and carry Davy in, in their arms. They would bring in a record player and play him biting blues. They travelled right across London to see him, because in many things he had been their mentor – not in drug-taking, but in intelligent understanding of experience and in gentleness. The nurses looked at them with suspicion and contempt.

He came out 'cured'. Then he got 'busted' several times (maybe he really did have marihuana; maybe he really did have heroin; or maybe he was just dead easy to pull in) and his wife, who had been fighting with her respectable West Indian family about Davy's welfare, phoned me to say 'they' wanted to take Davy away from her and put him in care. I had helped her before, in company with a sympathetic warm-hearted children's officer; but this time the children's officer had resigned in protest against bureaucratic officials, and I – only a writer with nothing to resign from – was just going into hospital. So I don't know what happened to Davy. Perhaps he is in an institution now. But at least he had nearly three years of intermittent exploring among the chaos and the warnings, and perhaps no one can entirely take that away from him.

Two children, and their parents. Compare them with the two children I described earlier – the child in the garden, and the child in the hotel – and you are comparing the unorganized distortion which characterizes the working class with the organized distortion which characterizes the middle class. Working-class people believe in 'luck', middle-class people believe in 'control'; each is the approved euphemism for a battered and chained identity. Working-class children get pushed too hard, get violent, and maybe get sent to Borstal. Middle-class children get pushed too hard, and maybe go schizophrenic or autistic, and – having been trained to be competent – make their own cage.

The only one of these parents who ever saw the child in front of him was Steve, and sometimes he was seeing the self he might have been, and anyway he couldn't keep his eyes open long enough because of his own pain, although he did try.

17

In a South London school I sat down at a table with four seven-year-old girls. Another little girl came up to me – bringing a list of very neat and carefully written words to show me. They must have been copied off pictures on the wall. The first word was *yarn*. Truly.

'Do you know what this word is?' I asked her

'Wool,' she said brightly.

The second word was *yacht*.

'And do you know what this is?' I said.

'Sailing boat,' she said brightly.

'Well, love,' I said, pulling her down next to me and putting my arm round her, 'it's really "yarn" and "yacht". . . . But never mind, you all tell me what are *important* words, and I'll write them all down.'

And without a second's hesitation, right round that table went 'ambulance' – 'dead' – 'dying' – 'nearly dead'. Now a slight pause. Then, quickly again, 'hospital' – 'doctors' – 'nurses'.

'Oh,' I said, 'has someone you know died then?' A child on my right said, 'My Nan's died. Died on Tuesday. I saw her in her coffin. But I didn't go to the funeral. Our Linda went.'

'Who's Linda?' I said.

'Her big sister,' said her friend.

'Linda looks after us,' said the first child.

'Where's your Mum then?' I asked.

'She ran away.'

''Cos she couldn't stand the row,' said her friend.

'And where's your Dad?'

'He's dead.'

All this completely matter-of-fact. Yarn . . . yachts . . . John, see the boats. . . . And the important words are 'dead' – 'dying' – 'nearly dead'.

I think what I find most extraordinary of all is that if I tell people this they think I am being depressing.

At the end of 1966 I wrote six stories about a large family such as might live in the East End of London – stories that in structure would make a six or seven year old's first read-for-yourself book, but with real conversation, real emotions, real people – and I took them to a school in the East End and read them aloud to a class of seven year olds.

The effect was extraordinary. The children began to laugh. They laughed physically, like a very small child laughs – helplessly. They laughed till the tears streamed down their faces. They couldn't sit down. They stood up and jumped up and down, hugging themselves . . . and hugging their neighbours. At first I thought I would wait till the laughter subsided before I read on, but the laughter never subsided. As I finished each one, they demanded the next. I read one after the other, marvelling all the time at the very young looseness and floppiness the children's bodies had taken on, and the quite extraordinary quality of their constant laughter. I have often read stories to children, and they have often laughed, but not like this.

I was still puzzling over it when I got home. Waiting for me was a letter from a head in Kettering to whom I had sent a typescript of another story I'd written and his report of the scene in his classroom was identical. He said one boy, whose father was 'just the amiable layabout Dad of your story', was trying to explain to the boy next to him, whose father was a 'stern conscientious worker-type', why the story was so funny and so important to him, but was laughing so much he could only jump up and down, tears streaming down his cheeks and gasp out, 'It's my Dad! It's my Dad!'

Standing with his letter in my hand and considering all this, my mind went back to the evening I had seen the play *Billy Liar* in a West-End theatre. 'Seen' is accurate since I could scarcely hear a word. I was extremely annoyed at the time. The laughter was continuous, drowning all dialogue, and completely physical; I came out of that theatre not only angry and frustrated since I love the play, but bruised all over from the helpless backslapping and knee-thumping I'd been subjected to from delirious hefty strangers. (It was at this time that Albert Finney, playing

Billy, who understood the phenomenon as little as I did
then, walked to the footlights and told them furiously if they
didn't shut up he was going home. The press discussed this quite
a bit at the time – such an event was unprecedented.)

Now I put the three experiences together, and it suddenly
clicked. The physical laughter of release from tension, the
laughter of acceptance, of recognition. For the first time with a
shock of joy those children, and those adults, had seen themselves
portrayed in preserves that hitherto were middle-class and alien.
They didn't have to pretend to be someone else any more. They
were released.

Heads wrote in about these books, scandalized and vehement,
from both middle-class and slum areas. Such subjects, they said,
should not be mentioned. Such subjects did not exist. Children do
not play on bomb-sites or dumps. There are no bomb-sites or
dumps. They have all been built over long ago (this was the beginning of 1967). All children play in parks or pleasant play areas.

All homes have hot and cold water and proper bathrooms, and nobody uses tin baths. Fish and chips must not be mentioned. No children play in old cars. The head of the family must not be held up to criticism.

It was evident that some heads flatly denied their pupils' identity. Also they had no sense of humour.

I took one of the stories, *Lesley's Story*, to a lively and flexible primary school near here, run by a head who has vitality, humanity and optimism. Nina has a job there. I read it aloud. On the edge of this concentrated group, Len was playing up, trying to enlist his friend's support and break up the reading by echoing the end of each sentence. Len is one of ten kids. His mother, the only person who has given the children affection, has finally abandoned them. They are now looked after when at all by the eldest sister, who lives at home with her illegitimate baby. Father has brought another woman home, but she is only a bedmate.

'Lesley,' I read. And every time, 'Lesbian,' echoed seven-year-old Len provocatively. Nina and I tried not to catch each other's eye, not wanting to laugh. I went on reading, and eventually he ran out of the group. But afterwards Nina said to me, 'So who says that child's not intelligent, and is incapable of reading – when he knows that Lesley and Lesbian start with the same syllable!'

I have just heard Len is no longer at this school. He is in care.

18

'These children have no experience,' teachers often say, with disdain, despair, compassion or charity.

But how can anyone 'have no experience'?

Here is Marion, age five, writing (or rather, dictating) a story.

Once upon a time there was a little girl called Janet Parkes. One day Janet Parkes was ill. Her mother called the doctor, and he said she would have to stay ill and die. One day Janet Parkes died and her mother cried and her mother took her to the grave. Janet's mother had another baby and he was a boy. She forgot about Janet. Janet's mother dreamed about Janet when she died, and those dreams made her sick. One day Janet Parkes came to life again, and her mother was so happy that she had her little girl back.

Is there no 'experience' in that piece of universal art?

Once I looked very quietly into our sitting-room, and there was a three year old called Sally and a twenty year old called Sarah sitting on the settee together. Sarah was softly playing her guitar and singing. Then she said to Sally, 'You sing, and I'll play to your song.' So Sally began to create in song, set free on a poetic mythological plane by music, and followed by Sarah she sang about being in a dark house frightened by strange sounds. . . . '"It was only the owl, only the owl," they said. . . . but I'm frightened, frightened by the dark, frightened by the owl, frightened because I'm alone in a dark house. . . .' It was a very long song, strange and beautiful and moving. I wished I could set a tape recorder going; I daren't even move to get pencil and paper because I was afraid of disturbing the spell that Sally was weaving.

Marion was in her first year at school, and Janet Parkes, a child in the same class, had told her that her Mummy had had a new baby and had touched something off in Marion's mind. As for Sally, she had known no father, her beloved brother was in prison, and a year ago her mother had been taken to hospital in the middle of the night while Sally was still sleeping, and Sally had wakened to an empty house.

Marion and Gary and some others, all now six, made up a story together. I just gave them the first line to start them off. They made it very realistic. '. . . And the children sat down, muttering and moaning, sticking their tongues out occasionally. . . .' Next week Gary finished it and gave it a wake-up-from-a-dream ending, with the children saying ' " You cruel liar. You're not our real Mummy. Our real Mummy went to the shops, and she was going to buy a present for one of our birthdays." "*My* birthday! I'll be seven on my birthday!" "And it was our wicked stepmother who said we had no money and we had to have spaghetti. And our real mother will be back at two o'clock." '

I was disappointed at losing the realism. I'll get it written in one go next time, I decided. Then, a teacher asked me casually who had come for my group. 'Gary? Oh, he's the kid who's adopted.'

Why do we try to lay down what is 'experience' and what is not? Why do we so rigidly try to separate 'realism' and 'fantasy'? The spontaneously invented games of a three year old are not elves and fairies but 'mothers-and-fathers', 'doctors', and later 'school' (are they fantasy or realism?). Fantasy is an exploration of living reality, and play a rehearsal of living reality, and we use them both as tools of growth that will help us first understand our reality, and then help us shape it with awareness and competence. (Is it surprising that people who live least effectively, creatively and absorbedly are those who have been allowed least play, least fantasy, self-expression, exploration?)

Marion writes a great deal.

How did it happen? Nobody knows. Only Marion and Eleanor know, and this is how we know. We once left our satchels at school by mistake and we had to go back to school to get them and it was then that we stopped to listen. And we heard a very queer sound. A scuffling sound. And Eleanor said 'Help! It is a ghost!' – because she once saw a ghost in church, but I do not believe in ghosts, but I still feel creepy about creepy sounds. I just said, 'Do not be silly. You are the silliest girl I ever met.'

But I was scared really, scared stiff. I could not stand it, but I dared not tell Eleanor.

That in fact was inspired by a burglary at school, discovered in the morning; but does that settle for us whether it is 'realism' or 'fantasy', and whether Marion has any 'experience'? And about the same time, after Bonfire Night, she wrote a picture-story, that is, drawings with captions:

As Victoria watched the bonfire the guy smiled with a mysterious look in his eyes and then he slowly burned away. In the night Victoria had a dream and she woke up in the night and she cried. In the morning she said she saw a big horrid man and she said she would draw him, and she scribbled and we laughed. Now what was happening? The guy was a magic guy and he had found out that Victoria liked him and he had been wondering why she had not tried to save him from being burned, and that was what had caused all the trouble. And as the wicked guy cackled wickedly to himself, now he was a wicked, mean and selfish guy. Instead of Johnny the good guy he was now Johnny the bad guy. Now he was trying to kill Victoria. He had tried to frighten her to death because he was sure that she was easily frightened, and he was a little bit right and a little bit wrong, because she was easily frightened but she could not be killed because of it. And here she is being frightened.

Marion and Sally are still in touch with their own roots, feeling through their unique personal experience what they do not yet know is their healing universality. How many teachers dare to be so much in touch?

I remember a poem by Christine Economides, a fourteen-year-old Greek girl at Risinghill School, Islington:

Loneliness
Sitting and waiting for someone to ring.
Waiting is for people who are ill or old,
But I am young.

This is the kind of statement that elicits instantly from many teachers (who perhaps are ill or old) the snappy comment, 'Nonsense!'

'They have no experience . . .' Years ago, I sometimes reluctantly judged children's poetry competitions. The subject set was invariably 'Spring' or 'Autumn', and the verses by these London children would be about skipping lambs, or migrating birds – such a sad conformist unfelt similarity, one could almost see the word l-a-m-b spelt out on the blackboard. Most of these children can't even keep a cat or a budgie in their Council flat. Some of them live in districts where there isn't one blade of grass. They have never seen a lamb in their life, skipping or static.

But the seasons still move for them – the sky still changes, the wind blows, harshly from the east or tenderly from the west. Why is their own experience treated with such indifference, such contempt? Isn't it valid?

For London children, autumn is throwing up sticks to bring down the conkers, it is slanting sunlight on tree trunks conker-red, it is bonfires and catherine wheels, crisp-curled golden-brown leaves lying on the common like brandy-snaps in shop windows, white mists and yellow fog, and seagulls white on the grass and black on the sky, and queuing outside church halls for jumble sales in the early afternoon and warming your hands on a packet of chips in the evening.

Winter is hearing the dry scutter of skeleton leaves teetering on their tips across the pavement and the rusty creak of the gulls; it is bleak black windows, toffee apples, immobilization and imprisonment in flats and classrooms, the rasping sound of motor chains outside the window when eyes are still unopened; it is the crunch of shoes in the dazzling snow, and later the brown spattering slush of the busy road, the ducks floundering and slithering on the icy pond, and wretched frozen lavatories; it is warm cosy fires, or broken windows stuffed with rags, it is the time when old people's noses drip and they keep their coats on indoors, it is the time of presents and the talk of presents and sometimes the stealing to get or give presents everyone else is talking about.

Spring is the swamp of the melting common, the first almond tree in the suburban street, tadpoles in a swinging jar, the baby sparrow fallen to the pavement, a crow lurching raggedly across the grass like a meths drinker, daffodils in the town-hall windows, strange furry silky catkins in the market under the railway arches, newspapers blown off stalls and flapping frenziedly round people's legs, gorse on the common with bird's-foot trefoil clustering under (a hen with chickens); it is Easter eggs in the shop windows, silly pigeons dropping twig after twig as they try to build an impossible nest on air (cooing like outraged dowagers or compassionate television interviewers) and sometimes, in the park, the thin cheep of invisible baby birds.

And summer is gay frocks and shirts, splashing in the paddling pool, sometimes dry-skinned and golden, sometimes sticky with

sweat and grime and ice cream, being chased away because you are the wrong age though the baby you are looking after is the right age. It is the time when the washing dries early, the time when the coach trip goes off, the time when fourteen people cram into the van and go to Southend. It is the different greens of the different grass and the different greens of the trees, the dogs wildly barking as the kite comes down, the smell of oranges, drains, melting tar, and the ecstatically sweet cut grass before the keeper chases you away. These and many many more, that vary from child to child and from district to district, each as important in its uniqueness and personalness as in its universality. A whole poem devoted to the filth of a frozen school lavatory or the extraordinary smell of a street drain, with every adjective carefully selected – that is experience. But those skipping lambs, those leaving and returning swallows, presented in neat, dead, pretty words, like cute little bridesmaid's posies, no.

A fifteen year old from Islington gave a mock talk on 'her vacation'.

Last year my Mum and Dad didn't have much money so we decided to take our vacation down the sewers. As there was a manhole outside the front door we didn't have to pay for the transport. As soon as we entered I could smell the aroma. It was a beautiful smell. On the walls there was a green substance which my very educated mother told me was called slime. We took plenty of things with us, and as we didn't have a suitcase we took them all in my pencil case. There was plenty of room for such necessities as the television, front door and many others. We stayed afloat in the water for a while and then climbed up the wall for some more comfort. I plugged the television set into the water and sat agaze at it all through the night. After we had been down there for what seemed a few hours, my dog suggested that we go now as he wanted to get home to his Fido meat. I decided to take a souvenir with me so I put some of the perfume from the sewers into a few bottles and took them home with me. I handed them round to my relatives and to my surprise the next day I received letters saying that they had fainted. They have not been round to see me for ages now, and I am all on my own, so if you want some perfume please contact me straight away.

This sort of cool out-of-school clowning is also an emotional comment of a different kind, but equally one that many teachers would call 'Nonsense'. Yet it is in direct line with the old music-hall songs ('I live in Trafalgar Square, With four lions to guard me. . . .') that are certainly not cosy or charming whatever sentimentalists may say, and nor do they have the Jewish nerve-quivering self-mockery, but rather a latent physical aggressiveness that is quite formidable. Perhaps this is why some teachers call this sort of thing 'nonsense' – until it reaches classic status – and pretend that it shows, *proves* even, that children like this have 'no experience'.

But apart from the basic experience that is common to all children, many would think that children living in poor social conditions have much *more* 'experience' than the more protected middle-class ones . . . evictions, gang warfare, fathers in jail, mothers run away or in mental hospitals, another woman as Dad's bedmate, sister with a baby and no husband, floors crumbling and ceilings falling in, the wage packet spent at the dogs, Nan lying in the front room in her coffin. . . . And indeed the very teachers who say 'they have no experience' are the ones who would most quickly agree with this. So clearly what the teachers really mean is not that 'they have no experience', but that they have no 'approved' experience, no cosy well-bred tasteful experience that, talked about openly, would not disturb them, the teachers. Does their education consist then in denying experience, wiping out past, present and future . . . producing (because children need to be accepted and loved) compliance in some, with a constant undercurrent of anxiety which is reality stirring behind the door, and apathy in others, and anger and hate in others?

One way we might undo some of the harm we have done, and decondition children, is to teach teenagers to listen to their dreams. Every human being is a creator, an artist, for everyone dreams. But perhaps a teenager's dreams, searchingly looked at, might disturb teachers more than anything they ever write. For the dreamers have escaped from good taste, from school rules, and looking again at the real things that have happened are searching for truth and coming face to face with their own revolutionary wisdom.

Indeed, in the context we have now, perhaps Authority had better leave our dreams alone. They might defuse them.

19

A girl at our local grammar school brought this to a teacher who
no longer took her now that she was doing O-level work.

Spirit Lost

A cry . . . a plaintive weird cry. – The cry of a lost soul. Lost and
without love. A cry that is terror . . . terror at being left in a world that
is a world no more . . . for a world is no more when you are lost and
without love.

I go on my way. This, I say softly to myself, has nothing to do with
me. I repeat the words. – I repeat them over and over again. – It does
not concern me . . . it is not my business.

My key is in my pocket. I take it out and carefully unlock the door.
It is late . . . very late. I go to bed and I think of the cry. All night I think
of the cry. All night, every night. I think, but I still repeat to myself the
words that are so untrue . . . it does not concern me . . . it is not my
business. . . .

It is dark . . . it is late. Again I hear the cry. The cry that is filled
with forlorn hopelessness. I look round. People are everywhere. Can
they not hear the cry? Can they not hear the cry that has invaded my
life? Why is it only I who can hear the hauntingly sad cry?

Oh foolish, sad one. . . . You realize not that it is your own soul crying
out . . . crying out for hope and love . . . and recognition.

Oh sorrowful one, for you hope is gone forever. You ignored the
cry, and so cut off the life of your spirit. Now will your spirit never
roam the skies, to mingle with the elate and beautiful wind. Oh, you
foolish one!

You are lost. The cry comes only once in your life. Why did you ignore
it? The cry you hear now is an echo only. An echo forlorn . . . dejected.
An echo to remind you of that which you have lost. . . .

A few months later, when she was fifteen I read through her
school book of essays, written for her O-level English teacher.
I was immediately gripped by the intensity of hate in her. Not
that it was expressed as such. What she expressed was an obsession
with lying (lies must be plausible to be 'good' . . . how can you be
sure that yours are plausible enough? . . . how terrifying it is not
to be sure . . . and, later on, how contemptible are people whose

lies are not good enough! . . .) and a quite desperate demand for punishment. She hated Holden Caulfield, she said (the earlier teacher had lent her *Catcher in the Rye*), and stated gratuitously 'his parents should have given him a good hiding the minute he started horsing around' and a little further down the page insisted 'murderers should be killed in case they kill someone else'. In this essay, her writing suddenly sloped backward in a startling tense way as if she were afraid of where she was going. The last sentence was pathetic, still hoping for help but too listless to be a plea, 'But these are only my views and I would not try to influence anyone else by them.'

Her O-level teacher responded throughout this very disturbed piece of writing by scathing comments on her punctuation and sentence structure. Nothing else, except an occasional 'Stupid!'

A little while after this the girl was expelled, for lateness. Her father was ill, there were brothers and sisters, and she was her mother's domestic help. She had written about clocks in her 'Spirit Lost'. 'You belong to a world from which I am separated. A world of people – people, who have assignments to carry out – people, with patterns to follow – people, with heads, not hearts.'

20

'I can't say like some people do, "Well, maybe it didn't do me much good, but maybe it did other people good."

'When I ran away from school, I was only eight, but I'll never forget it. I've often wanted to make a film about it. I started to write it down, but all these memories came rushing back and I couldn't face them. I had to put my pen down. I knew I couldn't do it.

'It's done me so much damage – I'll never get away from this. I want to take a machine-gun to the place.

'I'm not a violent person. But I just want to take it apart. I can't imagine in the whole of the rest of my life ever experiencing anything so terrible. Because it's so hopeless. You feel everyone is against you – you're on your own.

'I ran ten miles across Bristol to get away from school. It's a long way for a kid of eight. There was no one in, and I sat on the step crying. The head came in his car after me – it was a cul-de-sac. He got me in his car and he talked to me quite kindly, and then he took me back. And after a few days I was beaten.

'One thing I'll never forget. When I was about twelve, our maths teacher was ill and he was away for weeks, and we had another teacher. And we were all having this class with this other chap, and this first chap must have got better because suddenly the door was flung open and he came in.

'And the chap next to me, my friend, looked up and quite spontaneously he said "Oh, hello, sir!" And this teacher walked right across the room and gave him a terrific clip across the ear.

'I nearly shot up to the ceiling. And you think that because the boy's been given a clip, you must know that he's done something terribly wrong. I've never forgotten it. I think now – "You *bastard*!"

'The thickest boys came through. It was the law of the jungle. A sensitive boy was absolutely broken, just weeping his heart out, utterly humiliated and on the floor. There were many times when I was literally going out of my mind.

'One of our masters used to do flying at the weekend. He had a pilot's licence. And one weekend he was killed. And when we were told at school, I remember one boy saying, "Old Bloody Barton's gone at last! Thought we'd never get rid of him. Wonder who we'll get next." I couldn't believe it. This was a human being they were talking about. . . .

' "Bloody awful," he'd say. "Bloody awful!" And he'd shy your work back at you and it would fly past you and go underneath your desk and you'd have to scrabble about for it. "You've got no bloody idea!" That's why we called him "Bloody Barton". You know – "so much garbage, and I had to sit and read that crap when I could have been listening to my stereo record player".

'So I gave up trying to learn anything, and began to try to learn how to please the teachers and not get anyone shouting at you.

'And then suddenly you leave the school, and suddenly realize you can start putting your enthusiasm into practice, and suddenly you say, "They were wrong and I was right! I *do* have something to give!"

'But their conditioning was very thorough. And in emotional stress I still have nightmares that I'm back at school, and whatever emotional stress I'm in I'm thankful to wake up to it, out of that nightmare. I'll never shake it now.

'When you're seven, a day is a very long time. And one day stretches out after another, nine and a half years of it. And you don't ever know what you've done wrong, and you know you can never put it right.

'My biggest fears are not of dying. I wouldn't be afraid of being hanged. I wouldn't be afraid of being killed if the B B C sent me to Vietnam. I'm only afraid of going to prison. Because then I would feel I was back at school.'

He was very gentle and quiet normally. One night he suddenly burst out with this. I took it for granted he was talking about an approved school. But it turned out to be a public school.

It seemed his grandfather made some money, and decided his grandsons should have the education he never had. 'He was a very generous man,' my friend said.

'Did you ever tell him what it was like?'

'Oh no. I couldn't tell him. He meant well, and it would have hurt him.'

Some time ago, I asked another friend what he remembered most vividly from his school, what he instantly associated with it. He said at once, 'Violence. The only time I got smashed up really bad was at school. Every day you came you knew there was a possibility of getting smashed up really badly. And when we were made prefects, we knew that every time we asserted our authority, so called, we were in danger. The teachers who used corporal punishment or threatened us, and the teachers who were over-kind and didn't want us to grow up, we had just contempt for. There were a few, a very few, who treated you on their own level.'

I was very struck by this, because I had marked the same perceptiveness about teachers among the Risinghill pupils, but *Risinghill* hadn't yet been published. Schoolchildren, until they have been educated out of it (some of them never are, and probably become writers or schizophrenics), refuse to accept disguises.

I remember how Nina and her friends, when they were seven, used to talk about the teachers changing into witches and back again. At first I was amused by the 'fantasy' and flippancy of it, but as they talked the underlying seriousness and perceptiveness of the symbolism grew louder – I think this was the first time the natural basic element of mythology came home to me – and I saw how aware these small girls were of the disguises slipped on and off by self-righteous people. Many years later, when I worked on *Risinghill*, and unearthed many extraordinary episodes that I didn't mention in the book, I thought back to these little girls and their 'fantasizing'. We all of us go in for disguises at times, but it is a pity if the profession which spends all its time with children believes in permanent disguise, for children are by nature very close to mythology and speak the language.

I asked another young chap, also working at the BBC, what he remembered of his school, and he thought just a second or two and said, 'The whole of my education was directed to getting me to hate my parents. And what a triumph! When I finally graduated and they came to the ceremony, I didn't introduce them to anyone, and I was bitterly ashamed of them.'

So then I asked Bob what he remembered and he said with sudden bitterness, 'They treated you like shit. They told you you were shit, and they went on telling you, until in the end you believed them.'

One public school, one secondary modern and two 'good' grammar schools.

Then I talked to Pete. At first he talked about home – his father who drove him nearly round the bend. 'He's always on at me to get a job. He's always saying how he's worked *twenty years* ticket-collecting for London Transport. Well, that's all right. O.K. If you want to work twenty years ticket-collecting, well O.K. But he moans all the time about it, day and night. And then he expects *me* to do it and says he's ashamed if I don't!'

And later he talked about his education. He learnt nothing at school. For one thing, he was hardly ever there. His mother could never stay in the same place for long, so the family was constantly moving and Pete was always changing to another school, among strangers. He was a shy child. Teachers used to make him 'stand

up and say things', so that he always felt they meant him to be condemned out of his own mouth. His compositions were very incoherent; and one teacher, to emphasize deliberately that they were the worst and most senseless he had ever seen and thereby get the rest of the class 'with' him, used to make Pete stand up and read them out.

Pete would run away from school. The truant officer would find him and bring him back, and he would be caned and run away again. He left school, legally, as soon as he possibly could. And then at last he began to learn.

This is true of vast numbers of our children; in fact it may be still true of most of them. Only when they leave school do they begin to learn. I sometimes think we are simply taking a chunk out of their lives – ten years when we drive them and beat them

and disintegrate them and undermine them, till at last they can escape from us; and all they have ever learnt that is going to be any good to them and that will compensate for ten years of legal captivity is the bare technique of reading – not the pleasure in reading nor the companionship of books which luckier children learn before they come to school, but just the bare painful technique, and some children only learn that when they escape into life.

Pete now writes poetry. When he escaped from school – and after, I think, he spent some time in a detention centre – he met people who wrote, who played musical instruments, who talked and listened. 'I was all closed up. I got nothing out of school – just a rough idea of reading, really rough. But afterwards I met all kinds of people and everything opened up.'

21

Some years ago, well before the Act, a girl telephoned. 'You don't know me. I'm in trouble. Can I come to see you? Now.' That always meant 'I need an abortion'.

She was twenty miles away, with a girlfriend in a phone box. She had my address, phone number and full directions with a sketch-map in her pocket. I was on the grapevine.

Mary was in her early twenties. She was already three months pregnant, so an abortion was out. But her boyfriend was travelling over a hundred miles every weekend to see her, and there seemed to be a tenderness, a concern and a reliability in the relationship. She said they intended to marry, but not till she had finished her course.

We went into the possibilities. I phoned the London Education Authority because someone had told Mary she would have to pay back all her grant if she left her course; and they told me what they knew of other education authorities' policy in such matters, and of the policy of college principals in granting leave of absence. With such information, the three of us worked out a possible programme.

When the girls left, not only did the future seem to have a possible, controllable shape and even a potential glory (I use the word seriously), but Mary had discovered – casually, almost – something of tremendous importance to her: that it was possible to trust older people.

Back at her friend's home where she was staying, this tightly controlled girl, whose only safety had seemed to be in secrecy, told her friend's parents; and they were very kind to her. She was so enchanted and delighted – not merely with the actual happening, but with the confirming testimony it bore – that she rang me up to tell me.

She then decided to tell her own parents – to go back with John to her own home and tell them that she and John were marrying, they were having a baby, and that they had everything worked out and knew they could manage. When she phoned me that day, John was already on his way down to her.

I didn't hear from her again. At first I worried. Then I thought, it was just that her parents had taken over, and everything was fine.

So it rested. A year later, Ruth, her friend, came to see me.

From Ruth I learnt that Mary's parents had thrown John out when they came with their plans, that although he wrote, phoned, rang the front-door bell, they wouldn't let him see or speak to Mary, nor Mary communicate with him; that a month before the baby was due, they had her operated on, ostensibly for appendicitis, had her appendix and the baby removed, and the baby instantly adopted. They allowed John, Mary's lover and the baby's father, to know nothing of any of this. He and Mary did not see each other again, until a little while ago when they had met through Ruth's connivance, and had nothing to say to each other. What indeed could they say in a relationship criss-crossed and numbed by so many betrayals?

But I've told this out of turn. Before Ruth arrived, she made the usual phone call.

'. . . I came to see you last year, with another girl . . . I'm in the same trouble. Can I come now? With my boyfriend?'

So they both came. And when I suggested Ruth's parents might help, they both said emphatically no. So I said innocently, knowing nothing, 'But they were very kind to Mary, weren't they?'

'But Mary wasn't their daughter,' Ruth said. 'When it's your own daughter, it's a different matter.'

And that is how I came to hear what happened to Mary.

I wrote about Mary and Ruth in the *Guardian*, and was sent a letter by someone who said she had 'had bitter personal experience similar to that in your article'.

. . . Of course it is easy for outsiders to be kind. The reason is plain. This is a matter concerning family relationships. If the young people are prepared to throw overboard consideration for their families, well that is it, but don't deceive them into thinking that there is not a price to be paid. If parents are treated as of no account, no one should be surprised if they resent it, and act in the light of their knowledge of the situation.

It is important to bring home to the young people concerned that we are members of a social group, of a family, and that their conduct is not their own concern only. Ruth has not apparently learnt from her friend about her duty to the society in which she lives and which supports her.

Is it really so much a child needs – the right to have space, and time for exploration, so that each can grow at its own rhythm and become part of society in a natural way . . . to feel what they feel, to have their experiences accepted as valid, and to be responded to in their own context . . . to live lives that are their own, not someone else's . . . the right to have happy parents, whom society accepts and values?

Is it really so much? It is indeed. Ask our society that sets each creative child on the conveyor belt, and deals it as it moves along a hammer-blow here and a twist there, till it becomes the anonymous mass component that the state needs, and see society's response . . . see its priorities.

Yet each one of us is a member of 'society'. And only children, and the sheer brilliance of children, can save each one of us from the sickness and the death that we choose to call living.